ART FORMS
AND CIVIC LIFE
IN THE
LATE ROMAN EMPIRE

ART
FORMS
AND
CIVIC LIFE

IN THE
LATE ROMAN EMPIRE

By H. P. L'ORANGE

PRINCETON, NEW JERSEY
PRINCETON UNIVERSITY PRESS

Copyright © 1965 Princeton University Press

ALL RIGHTS RESERVED

L. C. Card: 65-10831

ISBN 0-691-00305-X (paperback edn.)

ISBN 0-691-03802-3 (hardcover edn.)

This book is a translation from the Norwegian
of *Fra Pricipat til Dominat*, published simultaneously
in 1958 by H. Aschehoug & Co.
(W. Nygaard), Oslo, Norway, and P.A. Norstedt &
Söners Förlag, Stockholm, Sweden

First PRINCETON PAPERBACK Edition, 1972

Princeton University Press books are printed on acid-free paper
and meet the guidelines for permanence and durability of the
Committee on Production Guidelines for Book Longevity of the
Council on Library Resources

Publication of this book has been aided
by the Whitney Darrow Publication Reserve Fund
of Princeton University Press

Printed in the United States of America

16   15   14   13   12   11   10   9

FOREWORD

AT AN early point in my studies of Late Antiquity I was struck by the marked similarity between the way in which the late antique state was organized and the predominating types of composition in both the figurative art and the architecture of that period. In my writings over the approximately thirty years I have devoted to the study of Late Antiquity, I have repeatedly drawn attention to the fact that the disintegration of the traditional society of the earlier empire—the Principate— and the consequent establishment of a new order during the late antique empire—the Dominate—were accompanied in the realm of art around A.D. 300 by a corresponding disintegration of classical tradition and the emergence of a new form of expression. The same "system" expressed itself with the same structural patterns in the life of practical organization and in art.

In order to examine this problem on a broader basis and to undertake a comparative structural analysis as indicated above, I was granted in 1952 the Hoff-Farmand Scholarship by the University of Oslo. Circumstances led to interruptions and postponements which prevented me from completing the research until 1958. The work was published in Norwegian in 1958 with a grant from the Svenska Humanistiska Förbundet by P. A. Norstedt & Söners Förlag (Stockholm) and by H. Aschehoug & Co. (Oslo).

I wish to express my gratitude to the University of Oslo for the Hoff-Farmand Scholarship, to the Svenska Humanistiska Förbundet, to Princeton University Press, which in the present edition publishes the work in English, and finally to Professor Erik Sjöqvist and Professor Irving Lavin for their interest in the book and to Dr. and Mrs. Knut Berg, who generously translated it into English.

H. P. L.

ACKNOWLEDGMENTS

For objects owned by collections or museums, the proprietor supplied the photograph unless another source is acknowledged. In other cases, acknowledgment is made to the following:

Alinari: Figs. 10, 67
Alinari-Anderson: Figs. 17, 33, 35, 36, 51, 53
Deutsches Archaölogisches Institut, Rom: Figs. 2, 3, 18-21, 30, 32, 37-39, 42-47, 50, 60, 62-65
Fototeca Unione, Rome: Figs. 5-7, 9
Istituto di Norvegia in Roma: Fig. 15
Middelthon, C.: Fig. 34
Teigen, K.: Fig. 52
Vasari, Rome: Fig. 4

CONTENTS

STRUCTURAL CHANGES
IN LATE ANTIQUITY

I. CIVIC LIFE AND THE STATE

THE everyday life of the average man—his whole political, economic, and social life—was transformed during Late Antiquity. The free and natural forms of the early Empire, the multiplicity and the variation of life under a decentralized administration, was replaced by homogeneity and uniformity under an ever-present and increasingly more centralized hierarchy of civil officials. Characteristic of the earliest period of the Principate was the infinite variety in the modes of life on the local level, the vigorous natural growth of the towns, the provinces, and the land districts of the enormous Empire, the self-development and natural rounding-off of civic life in individual urban communities (*municipia*), each with its own municipal government and administration. Late Antiquity leveled and regulated these forms of free growth, the community organizations were absorbed into the compact, all-powerful state.

The equalization, standardization, and centralization had already begun under Trajan. Jurisdictionally, the provinces arose to the level of Italy, which gradually lost its preeminence. The development tended towards a complete equalization of all the Roman provinces. The imperial idea won out over the old city-state of Rome and the old national state of Italy. As early as Hadrian, the Roman army had been recruited from all the provinces of the realm, and simultaneous with this provincialization of the army, the border districts were Romanized, again a step toward uniformity. The *Constitutio Antoniniana* of Caracalla from A.D. 212, which gave Roman citizenship to all free subjects of the Empire, is a confirmation of this new situation.

In the field of practical organization this advancing equalization of powers, this leveling, and this massive consolidation of all elements, becomes apparent above all in the relations between the state and the municipalities. The great wars of Trajan had been an economic strain which had disrupted the finances of the cities; the central administration, therefore, placed imperial commissars in many municipalities to correct these disorders. Furthermore, ten-man committees were appointed by the city councils—*decemprimi* in the West, δεκάπρωτοι in the East—in order to enable the central power through such committees to intervene more quickly in the internal affairs of the municipality.[1] It was characteristic of the whole subsequent development that public offices in the municipalities—for example, the city councils and the ten-man committees—were burdened with state responsibilities, taking thereby the form of compulsory state service (what Romans called *munus* and Greeks, λειτουργία). This change in the character of the municipal office struck at the organic expression of the particular way of life in the world of classical antiquity—city government.[2] At the beginning of the third century A.D., great jurists such as Papinianus, Callistratus, Ulpianus, put into practice the theory of the municipal *munera* and gave this system its legal foundation.[3] City officials

---

[1] E. Kornemann, *Weltgeschichte des Mittelmeerraumes*, ii, Munich, 1949, p. 117.

[2] F. Oertel, *CAH*, xii, p. 259.

[3] In the *vita* of Antoninus Pius we read that the Emperor deprived a number of people who did not work of their wages, saying that there was nothing meaner and more heartless than the man who lived off the state without giving anything in return (*dicens nihil esse sordidius, immo crudelius, quam si rem publicam is adroderet qui nihil in eam suo labore conferret*). *Script. hist. aug., vita Pii, 7.* Here for the first time in world history is proclaimed the officially controlled duty of all citizens to work (Kornemann, *op.cit.*, p. 158). This is a step in the direction of state socialism, in sharp contrast to the individualism in economic theory of earlier times. "The replacement of one economic system by the other, and the substitution of a new civilization and

4

and wealthy council members now became personally responsible, in a way hitherto unknown, for the state revenue. Above all they were responsible with their personal fortunes for the collection of the taxes assessed in their city. Eventually, all who were not exempt in order to perform other state duties, such as military duty, had to take on municipal *munera*—financial, intellectual, physical, etc.—each according to his capacity and ability. Both the wealth and those who possessed it were bound to specific local *munera*, thereby becoming immovable.[4]

In so far as the free guilds (*collegia*) performed a vital task for the state, they too were encroached upon by the central authorities. They were now organized into corporations (*corpora*) and were obliged to render specific services to the state. The ship-owners (*navicularii*) and the corn-merchants thus were, for example, required to supply Rome with provisions, and the building trade had also to assume the duties of the fire brigade. Freedom of work was thus replaced by the obligation to work for the state and, through the transformation of the free trades into hereditary *munus*, people became bound to their professions and to their dwelling places. A similar *immobilization* occurred also in the social and economic life of the rural population. On the large estates (*latifundia*) and on the enormous imperial domains, there emerged a new class of small tenant farmers (*coloni*), who became ascripted leaseholders under the landowners (*possessores*) or their vassals.[5]

The end result of this development was an unchangeable, firmly crystallized order. All classes, or at least all except the privileged class, were bound to their

---

attitude toward life for the old took more than a century and a half. It was completed by the end of the III century, but the beginnings go back to the earliest years of the II century" (Oertel, *op.cit.*, p. 256).

[4] Kornemann, *op.cit.*, p. 158.   [5] *Ibid.*, p. 159.

professions, "the peasant farmer to his land and forced labor, the state-employed worker to his workshop, the trader, including the *navicularius*, to his business or his corporation, the small property-owner to his duties in connection with the *munera*, the large property owner to the curia, the soldier to his military service, and so on."[6] The individual no longer lived independently but within the state. He was no longer seen in his natural environment within life's organic groupings, in lively harmony with his surroundings, but as a firmly incorporated immovable part in the cadre of the state. As with the individual, so also with the communities. The municipalities no longer lived within themselves, but in the state; we no longer see them in vigorous self-growth, but firmly incorporated into the great symmetrical order of the state. In contrast to the organic expansion based on the concrete and individual life, so to speak, along an elementary growth line reaching upward from below, we now find an orientation directed downward from above, a higher order descends and is implanted into the elements—"an orientation is imposed from above upon the whole social and economic order."[7] The characteristic feature of this higher order is the uniform simplification, the coordination of equal elements and the crystallic consolidation of the whole. Everywhere the finer social differentiations disappear and the sharp edges and the broad planes of the blocklike mass of the state break through. The rich articulation which distinguished the life of the Principate had been lost forever. The individuals and the natural civic organisms in which they were grouped, more and more seemed to disappear into the massive and monotonous formations envisioned by the central administration as supporting walls for the Dominate's state structure.

[6] Oertel, *op.cit.*, p. 268.   [7] *Ibid.*, pp. 254 ff.

6

Civic Life and the State

The increasing standardization and equalization of life, the blocklife fusion of the civic organisms, was revealed characteristically in the increasing militarization of society—indeed in the whole way of life. The soldier-emperors' simplification of the government according to a military pattern was followed by a general militarization of the civil service and an assimilation of the civil into martial law (*castrensis jurisdictio*).[8] The whole administration of the state was increasingly organized and conceived according to military categories. Civil service was regarded as military service. Every civil servant, from the highest to the lowest, counted as an officer or a soldier. In all *officia* (public office), there are, according to Lactantius, *milites* (soldiers), and their service is a *militia* (war service).[9] The wages for civil officials are *stipendia* (soldier's pay). Subordinate civil servants are *cohortales*, i.e., belonging to a *cohors* (a military detachment). As the civil service was commonly called *militia*, a new name—*militia armata*—had to be invented to distinguish military service.[10]

Such a martial conception regarding civil servants demonstrates that the state demanded the same discipline and obedience of its civil administration as that which was required of the army. Before the highest authority, the *dominus*, every form of protest is silenced. His bidding is a command to be obeyed blindly. The people subordinate themselves, each and every one without exception, *en bloc* to this command. It is this unconditional, mass obedience which suggests the associations with the soldier, the military unit, and thereby with the whole militaristic

[8] S. L. Miller, *CAH*, xii, pp. 28 ff.
[9] *De mort. pers.*, 31.
[10] W. Seston, *Dioclétien et la Tétrarchie*, Paris, 1946, pp. 347 f. (hereafter referred to as "Seston"); A. Alföldi, "Insignen und Tracht der römischen Kaiser," *Mitteilungen des Deutschen Archäolog. Instituts, Röm. Abt.*, 50, 1935, pp. 64 f.; Kornemann, *op.cit.*, pp. 257 f.

terminology. Even Christian obedience of the period expresses itself, characteristically enough, in this style; God's servants are *milites Christi*.

This military way of life, which also becomes apparent in the imperial art and architecture of the period, is in the strictest accord with the peculiar pattern of the Dominate. The military aspect of man, that is, exactly the aspect which binds him to rank and file, letting him disappear as a person into a number within a unit, into a solid block, into a sum of uniform elements. Militarization, therefore, marks the basic characteristic in the form structure of the Dominate, in sharp contrast to the earlier Empire. The contrast between the military and the civil orders is just the contrast between mechanical coordination and organic grouping, between the natural formations in free life and a massive alignment in rank and square, between individual, natural motions and movements *en bloc*. Both in community life and in art the large block formations and mass movements now appeared ever more clearly behind the continually thinning veil of traditional antique forms.

II. ARCHITECTURAL FORMS

THE same profound contrast between the Principate and the Dominate which we have found in organized society is also apparent in art. In this chapter we shall limit our comparisons to architecture, and the transformation of form, which takes place here, may be described briefly in the following way.

As the classical orders disintegrate during the Roman Empire, buildings lose their organic corporality, the clear articulation of their parts, and the functional relationships among them; they are gradually dissolved into a system of plain, simple walls. Here again, we see the characteristic transition from organic articulation of a well-differentiated structure to an abstract simplification in great planes and lines. To make this transformation clear it is first necessary to characterize the classical conception of architecture.

When the classical Greek fashioned something, he required of the form that it give the clearest possible expression of the object's particular function. A vase, for instance, is a container which has the special ability to enclose a liquid and hold its mass in balance. This function is physically expressed in the form of a Greek vase and is reflected in its decoration. No column is found in which the column's function—that of being a support—and no capital is found in which the capital's function—that of absorbing and transmuting pressure between the architrave and the column—is stamped with such objective clarity as in Greek architecture. One might say that the plastic form is brought forth from deep within the object itself. The form is organic, immanent.

Thus, the classical artist does not bring the form to an object from without or above, but brings it forth from

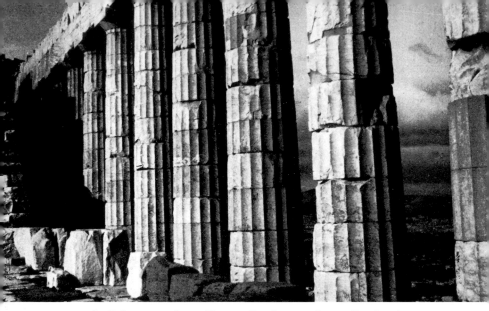

1. Columns and entablature, Parthenon, Acropolis of Athens

within the object itself. It is, therefore, characteristic of classical art that it is guided by the idea of a natural beauty inherent in the object; of a perfection which pervades the very smallest detail of it and which the artist, the architect, or the craftsman himself can bring forth from the object, and indeed can measure and determine numerically. Plutarch speaks of exactness of the beautiful: κάλλους ἀκρίβεια.[1] The classical architectural ornament can illustrate this conception (Figs. 1, 2).

Thus the constitution of ideal systems of proportion is a typical expression of classical art and architecture. From a given measure in the plan—for example, the distance from column to column—a number of other measurements can be determined: the proportions of the rafter system and thereby of the roof—even the proportions of sections of the building which are neither seen together with, nor are directly dependent on the columns. In the same way that the individual type of a

[1] Plutarch, Perikles, 13.

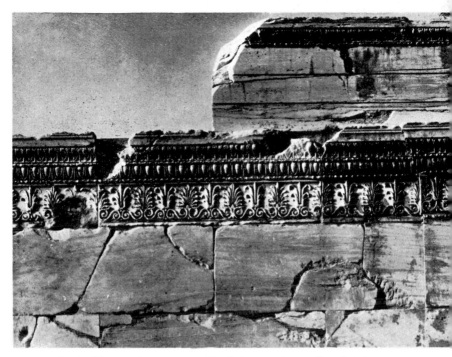

2. Architectural ornament, Erechtheum, Acropolis of Athens

living being determines the form of each single part of it, so the principle for the whole structure of the classical building is contained within each single element of it. In each of the three classical orders—the Doric, the Ionic, and the Corinthian—the building grows and unfolds in accordance with an organic law analogous to that which reigns in living nature.

It is precisely because the classical building is such an organic and self-sustained, such an autarchical, entity that it refuses to submit to larger architectural compositions. Often on sacred sites the classical temples stand with peculiar recalcitrance beside one another, each with its own orientation determined by its god or cult, by sacred portents and signs in the temple ground (Fig. 3). Each building defies superior order of axiality, symmetry, or unity of direction.

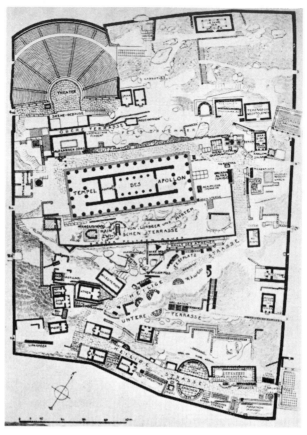

3. Delphi

This organic and autonomous life, this supreme development from within of each part, of each ornament of
the building, was lost during the Hellenistic-Roman
evolution which followed. The individual building was
continually subordinated to a dominating, all-embracing
architectural plan in which each structure is coordinated
in relation to the axis of the whole, thus becoming a
dependent part of a larger complex.[1] The axiality of the
layout, for instance of the imperial fora of Rome (Fig.
4), forces one into the central axis of the square where

[1] H. Kähler, *Wandlungen der antiken Form*, Munich, 1949, pp. 13 f.

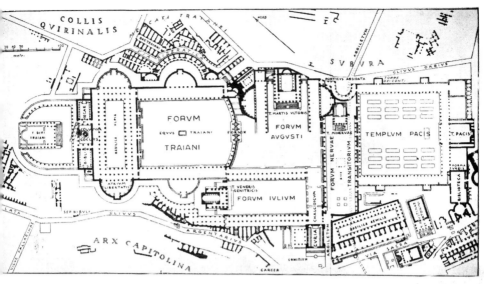

4. Imperial *fora* of Rome

one is faced by the towering temple façade.[2] The final
goal of this whole development was not reached until
Late Antiquity. We shall soon see how the Dominate
standardized, subordinated, and symmetrized all the single
building organisms in accordance with large and strict
axes of the whole architectural composition.

But with the subordination of the buildings to these
axes, the individual structural units dissolve and disappear
into the total architectural design; they lose their firm inner organization, their vivid proportionality, and the
clear articulation of their separate parts. Characteristic of
the whole development is the assimilation and mixing
together of the three classical building orders. Architectural decoration no longer depends upon an order that is
an organic system of ornament encompassing the whole
building.

Antiquity's sensitivity to the inner life of the architectural detail, its plastic beauty and expressiveness, gives
way (Fig. 13). The traditional décor, friezes and architec-

[2] H. Kähler, *op.cit.*, pp. 15 ff.

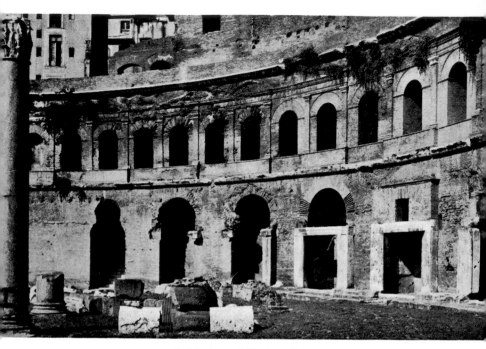

5. Market of Trajan, Rome

tural ornament, is absorbed more or less completely by the massive wall. The eye is no longer fixed upon the separate building parts. This is the reason why the flood of antique *spolia*, i.e., building parts taken from earlier monuments, are admitted into the architecture of Late Antiquity, where they may be reemployed for essentially different architectural purposes, unhampered by their original tectonic function. From around A.D. 300, and on into the Middle Ages, are thus put side by side building elements taken from utterly dissimilar monuments, belonging to the most diverse systems of ornamentation and having had widely different functions. It even happens, for example, that the bases of columns are used as capitals. And it must be emphasized that this did not occur during a period of technical falling-off, but during one of the most glorious epochs in the history of ancient architecture. The extensive use of *spolia* has, with good reason, been

14

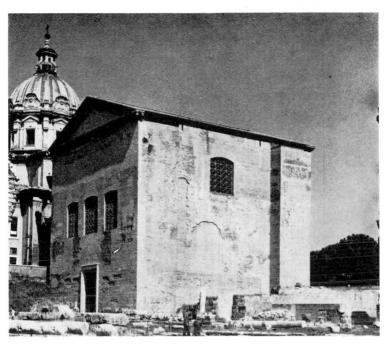

6. Curia of Diocletian, Rome

compared with the contemporary trend towards the use
of prefabricated building parts, especially capitals, which
are mass-produced without having originally been intended for any particular building. Like the *spolia*, these
prefabricated parts also often have to be cut or trimmed
before they can be placed in architectural bond. The point
of the matter is that the clearly defined form and function of each separate building element is no longer felt.
Undisturbed by arbitrarily cut elements or a helter-skelter
of undigested *spolia*, the eye glides over the architectural
forms, follows the great movements of the masses, the
grandiose rise of the vaults and the endless flights of
monotonously divided walls. Characteristically abstract,
peculiarly far-seeing and therefore summary, the glance
skips over detail and articulation in order to rest with
mass and dimension.

It is well known that during the Roman period—

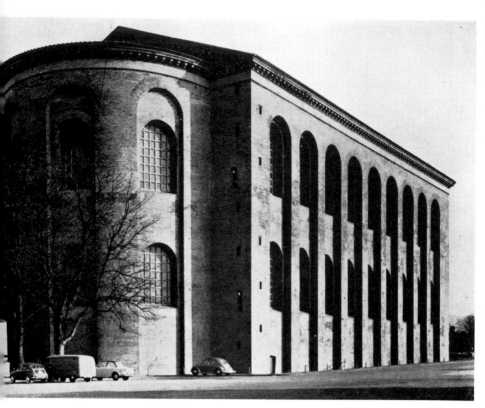

7. Basilica of Constantine, Trier

and particularly evident in the western world—a new system of construction came into use. In place of the traditional column-architrave architecture appears the new archivolt- or arcade-architecture. Characteristic of this architecture, until the end of the third century A.D., is the breaking up and articulation of the archivolt façade by the elements of the classical building orders, thus the arcades are enclosed in a frame-work of column-architrave architecture. This is the well-known system of which we have an early example in the Roman Tabularium (78 B.C.) and which is infinitely repeated in both monumental and utilitarian architecture; for example, in the brick façade of the Market di Trajan in Rome (Fig. 5). Where constructions in *opus quadratum* are concerned,

16

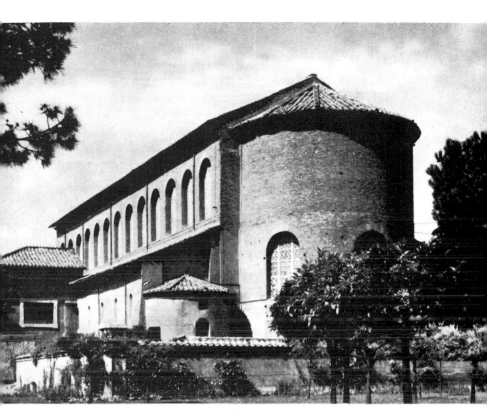

8. Santa Sabina, Rome, ca. A.D. 425

the elements of this décor are generally incorporated into
the wall itself with the half-columns and the flat beams
projecting only in low relief from the wall surface. However, especially in the second and the third century A.D.,
this architectural décor is separated from the walls with
detached columns supporting an entablature returned
back to the wall, thus appearing as a magnificent screen
in front of the building, as can be seen, for example, in
Roman triumphal arches. At the end of the third century
there was a strong reaction against this traditional system
of decoration. Especially in the West the splendid column
decoration vanishes and the classical articulation by
column and architrave more or less disappears from the
archivolt construction.

Structural Changes in Late Antiquity

Typical of the new architectural style are thus the large continuous wall surfaces, interrupted only by the functional wall-supports which, by more frequent repetition, give a firm, monotonous division of the wall through the regular and uniform passage along it of large arches and flat pilaster strips. In the Senate building of Diocletian at the Forum Romanum (Fig. 6), the great wall surface of the façade, crowned by a simple gable, is broken only by the portal and three large windows; strong corner pillars support the high walls. In Constantine's Basilica in Trier (Fig. 7, cf. Fig. 8), the outer walls are strengthened by arcadelike projections, which—as regular as the archivolts of an aqueduct and unrestrained by traditional decoration—run along the plain walls.[3]

Exactly as the architecture here throws off the traditional column-architrave decoration, the contemporary figurative art, as we shall see, drops the traditional patterns of composition. In contemporary portraiture the individual modeling sinks into the surface and the whole physiognomical complex is simplified into a crystalline regular totality, just as the plastic articulation of the building structure disappears into the great continuous wall surfaces.

[3] A. Boëthius has made fundamental studies in this late antique architecture in, for example, *Roman and Greek Town Architecture* (Göteborgs Högskolas Arsskrift, 54, 1948: 3); *Stadsbebyggelsen i Roms Hamnstad Ostia* (Göteborgs Högskolas Årsskrift, 57, 1951:2).

III. THE SPIRITUAL BACKGROUND

IN OUR comments upon architecture in the previous chapter the transformation of form appears mainly in a rather negative light: namely, the dissolution of the classical building structure. A positive side of this transformation is a new experience of space, a new feeling for the interior itself, which is an expression of the new spirit of the time. An appreciation of this positive side makes it possible for us to meet with a better understanding the peculiarly abstract—as it were, the distant glance which we have continually encountered in Late Antiquity.

It is of decisive importance that the large and simple wall surfaces of the new architectural style act as clearly defined space-enclosing boundaries in quite a different way from the much divided structural forms which they displace, thus in a new way making the unified interior manifest (Fig. 9). As the plastic decoration disappears into smooth walls, simple planes now enclose a clear and unified interior. It is in this interior that the eye now becomes immersed. Architecture becomes introspective. The building structure is reduced to a mere shell surrounding what is encompassed. It becomes no more than the enclosure of space.[1] Let us illustrate this with an example.

An important innovation which presumably first becomes common in the architecture of the third and fourth century—seen, for example, in the Christian basilica — is a continuous stretch of wall which now rises above the row of columns (Fig. 10). Such a construction is in conflict with the fundamental principles of classical archi-

[1] The new room architecture of the Empire is excellently described by G. von Kaschnitz-Weinberg, "Vergleichende Studien zur italisch-römischen Struktur," *Mitteilungen des Deutschen Archäolog. Instituts, Röm. Abt.*, 59, 1944, pp. 89 ff.

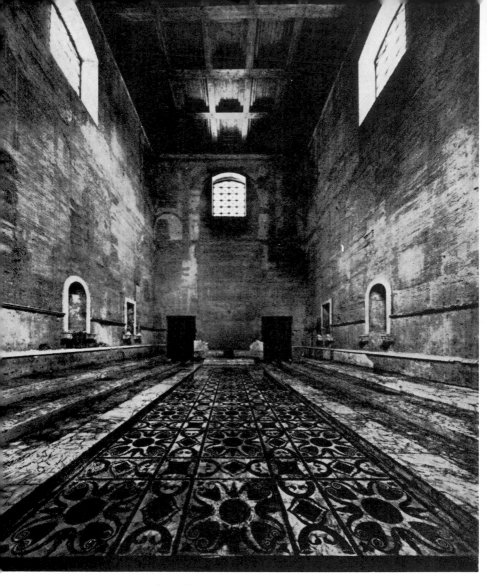

9. Interior of the Curia of Diocletian, Rome

tecture. The classical principle is to indicate the equilibrium of forces in the interaction between the supporting column and the heavy load of the architrave. A further construction above the rows of columns can, according

20

to the classical rule, only repeat this interplay between column and entablature, as seen, for instance, in the two-story rows of columns in the interior of the classical temple (Fig. 11). Now, with the massive wall replacing the organically muscular system of rows of columns and entablature recurring over one another, the classically organized building structure disappears behind a merely space-enclosing wall. The columns are withdrawn into the wall they support and are subordinated to the new crystalline totality of space. Everything now serves this interior. Above all, light is the space-creating element and models in its various intensities the different parts of the interior. In the Christian basilica, for example, the superstructure appears with radiant luminosity in contrast to the twilight of the lower zone which becomes even dimmer in the aisles.

In this transformation of the architectural forms during the Roman Empire we study in reality the profound human conversion from the "corporal beauty" of classical tradition to the transcendent contemplation indicative of the Middle Ages. One renounces the whole corporeal building—the columns, friezes, architectural ornament, the whole décor which Vitruvius still considered the *dignitas* of architecture—in order to immerse oneself in incorporeal space, in the insubstantial, intangible interior filled with light and shadow. From the clear, plastic definition of form one turns toward the realm of the abstract: a turning which, better than anything else, characterizes the whole attitude toward life in Late Antiquity.

Plastic art too is marked by this new attitude. It is thus significant that sculpture toward Late Antiquity adopts a technique that abolishes plastic form as such. While in classical times the whole modeling was accomplished by the chisel, one now finds a decidedly wider use of the

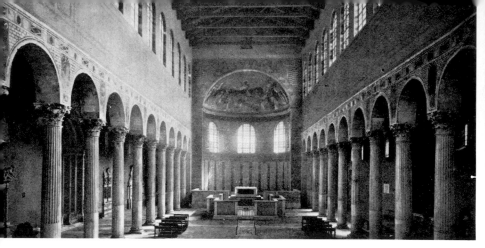

10. Interior of Santa Sabina, Rome, ca. A.D. 425

running drill. What does not such a change signify for the whole creative process! The chisel works out the tangible form, it follows flexibly all the ridges and hollows, all the ripples of the plastic surface (for example, Fig. 14). The drill on the other hand, works illusionally, it does not follow the tangible form but leaves a glimmer of lighted marble edges between sharp, shadow-dark drill grooves (for example, Figs. 22, 33, 34). With this technique the body loses its substantiality, it disintegrates: we are anxious lest it shrink to nothing and vanish. Also in architectural ornamentation we find this profound transformation of form. Examine, side by side (Figs. 12 and 13), an antae-capital from Didymaion by Milet, and a piece of a cornice, from the palace of Diocletian in Spalato;[2] compare the wonderful plastic, full-bodied egg-and-dart motif in the classical capital with the bodiless *clair-obscure* of the same ornament in the late antique cornice.

At the same time that the form thereby becomes increasingly insubstantial, it gradually loses its individual nature and becomes steadily more standardized, but with an ever more firmly crystallized significance. There is a

[2] Kähler, *op.cit.*, pl. 27a, pp. 60 ff.

22

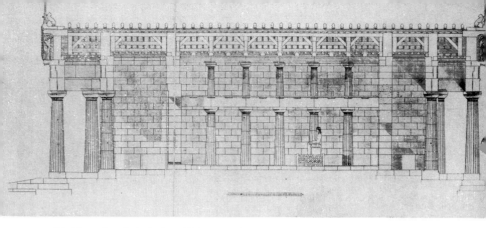

11. Temple of Aphaia, Aigina, early v cent. B.C., reconstruction
(Furtwängler)

movement away from lifelike nature to abstract types, from plastic articulation to conceptual generalization, from the corporeal to the symbolic. A higher meaning is implanted in the object, which more and more is reduced to a shell enclosing this meaningful core, more and more becomes a sign referring to a thought—and, as a sign, always identical, formula-like, stereotype.

Choose as an example such a central ornamental motif as the spiral rinceau of Late Antiquity and early mediaeval times (Fig. 15). It is now no longer a natural growth as it was in the classical tradition (Fig. 14): the stalk has become a lifeless band twining up into abstract, uniform circles, the whole plant an ornament without growth and lifelike nature. But this ornament encloses a new "interior," a new content, it has a life outside the order of nature; the rinceau blossoms forth into crosses, or it grows out of a chalice, or something similar, and thus becomes filled with new meaning. "I am the vine, ye are the branches" (John 5:15). As the vine loses its individual "object-nature," it becomes condensed to a symbol. It is precisely this which is characteristic of the transformation from Antiquity to the Middle Ages: the

23

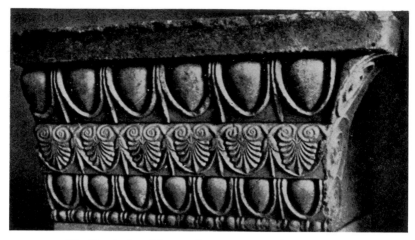

12. Classical architectural ornament, early v cent. B.C.

objects lose their natural substance, their bodily volume, their concrete lifelike reality, but in return enclose a new "interior," a meaningful core, they become symbols and conceptual expressions. It is as if the natural objects flee from living perception and as if in their flight they are contracted to increasingly summary and simplified figures until, in the end, they remain only as fixed points of meaning in the distance. These distant points of meaning, this multitude of stars in the sky of abstraction, is what Late Antiquity's distant glance is contemplating.

Look at the portrayal of man in the Middle Ages. Face and body are simplified to certain significant types; they become vehicles of certain symbols and signs, of certain fixed formulae of expression, of certain sacred attributes or certain insignia of state, all adhering to a higher and perpetual order into which the fleeting human being has entered. We choose as an example one of the well-known processions of saints represented on the nave walls of Sant'Apollinare Nuovo in Ravenna (Figs. 17, 67), and compare them with the famous imperial procession on the Ara Pacis from the time of Augustus (Fig.

24

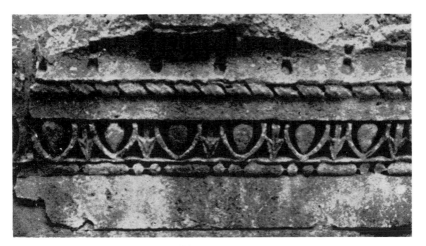

13. Late antique architectural ornament, ca. A.D. 300

16). Spiritlike and seemingly bodiless, the saints float past our eyes against a homogeneous background of symbolic palms of victory, each as a uniform element in an endless row: equal in height, with the same figure and with the same step, in the same venerable pallium costume, varied only in its detail, bearing the wreath of martyrdom, haloed, each of a singularly solemn, wide-eyed type which, for the beholder in Antiquity, was associated with the idea of man become divine (pp. 123 f.). Thus, the natural individuality recedes before a meaningful stereotype which characterizes the essence of the saints and indicates their place in an eternal hierarchical order. In the same way, the individualistic portraits of the emperors disappear, as we shall see (pp. 121 f.), in such depersonalized images, in a "sacred type" (τύπος ἱερός),[3] representing the Imperial Majesty itself. The emperors therefore become "alike" in the same way as the saints: the very idea of the *divina maiestas* penetrates and transforms the facial features. Man's image is formed according to suggestive formulas of expression, which

[3] τύπος ἱερός, in late antique literature and art: L'Orange, *Studien zur Geschichte des spätantiken Porträts*, Oslo, 1933, pp. 91 f.

25

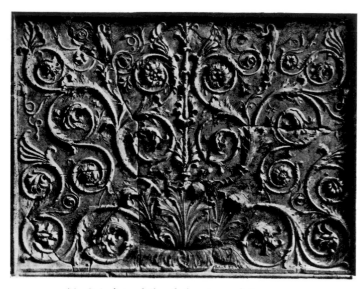

14. Spiral tendrils of the time of Augustus.
Detail from Ara Pacis, Rome

are associated with something higher and more essential than the individual himself. One may compare the stereotype character-masks of the antique theater, which "depict" the role played by the actor, and at the same time conceal the actor's personal features. We see men, not as lifelike individuals but in the role they play upon the stage of eternity. One's thoughts go to the late antique priests of the Eleusinian mysteries who, upon entering their office, gave up their names.

The inner meaning pierces through the natural exterior of an object and creates new formulas of expression and new patterns of composition. Instead of grouping the figures according to their natural order, they are now placed according to a pattern that allows their inner significance and their inner reciprocal relationship to be revealed. Especially characteristic of this trend, as we shall see, is the *Maiestas Domini* composition with all elements—men, architecture, etc.—placed symmetri-

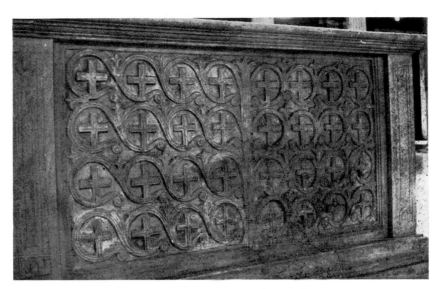

15. Early mediaeval spiral tendrils,
Santa Sabina, Rome

cally around God or emperor (pp. 101 ff.). Like the grouping of figures, their dimensions are also divorced from their natural relations to one another: the relative size of the figures does not correspond to their real measurements, but to their inner import and significance. Thus the form and action, the grouping and dimensions of the figures correspond to a reality in the realm of ideas, a function and a dignity in an eternal unchanging hierarchy of powers and orders.

The same shift of emphasis from the external to the internal appears at the same time in aesthetic theory. In the classical period, beauty is defined as proportionality: a proportionality which can be expressed in measures and numbers and thus is based upon the proportions of the human body (Polyclitus' Canon). This ideal of beauty applies to all fields of classical art, in sculpture as well as in architecture (pp. 21 ff.). A completely new aesthetic was developed during the third century: beauty does not re-

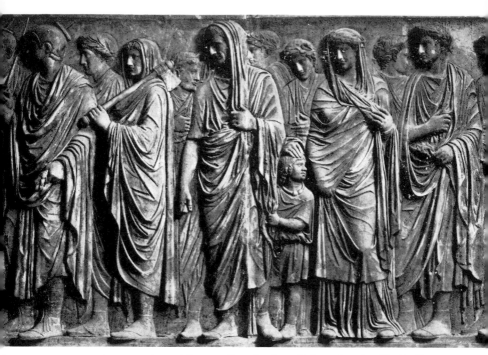

16. Procession of figures. Detail of a relief on the Ara Pacis, Rome

side in the proportions of the body, but in the soul which penetrates and illuminates it, that is, in expression (the Enneads of Plotinus). Beauty is a function of the inner being (τὸ ἔνδον εἶδος).

Also on the ethical level we are dealing with a revaluation and transformation of the classical attitude to life, an *Umwertung aller Werte*. And again the change is marked by a turning away from the external towards the internal world. The ideal is no longer what one could call proportionality of the soul, the harmonic organization of its natural energies with acceptance also of the instinctive and sensual life—the whole state of mind which is defined in the term σωφροσύνη. The goal is now a pure spiritual existence in faith and wisdom, an overcoming of the impulsive and sensual life, the body—

28

indeed, the whole outer world—consequently a concentration upon the inner life which shatters the traditional organic ethic of "a sound mind in a sound body." The hero of Late Antiquity is the martyr and the ascetic—the legends of martyrdom replace the heroic myths of classical times.[4]

The philosophy of Late Antiquity teaches that the natural sensual life—all life in the "flesh"—belongs to a lower form of existence. The aim is to free one's spirit, one's *pneuma*, from the natural man. The last great unifying religion of antique paganism, Neo-Platonism, systematizes this view. The soul, untouched by the material, is a celestial being; but through "a downfall into matter" it has materialized in a body and has been cast down into this world. In our natural existence here on earth the soul is therefore chained to a lower principle

[4] E. Lucius, *Die Anfänge des Heiligenkults*, Tübingen, 1904, *passim*.

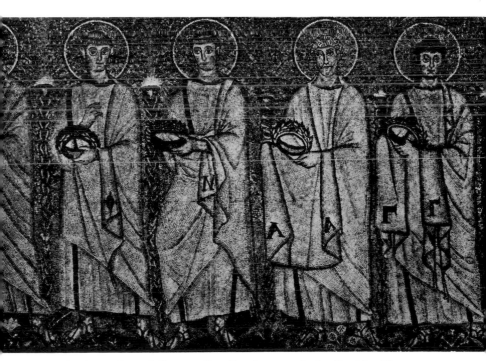

17. Procession of figures. Detail of a mosaic in Sant'Apollinare Nuovo, Ravenna. VI cent. A.D.

and left to the deceitful perceptions of the senses. The object is to liberate this heavenly being from matter and make it independent of the corporeal nature and sensuous apprehension. We must fight our way out of the chaos of feeling and imagination in which our senses ensnare us and strive for a higher reality, the eternal order behind the things of nature. Still in the middle of the third century A.D., Plotinus saw in the tangible reality of nature a beautiful reflection of the Ideas. However, at the beginning of the fourth century things of nature have lost this luster, they are now considered only a jungle of confusion where humans lose their way. One withdraws from the external and changeable world of illusions, from the things of nature, from "the body beautiful," and concentrates upon the abstractions of the inner life, upon symbols, ideas, and conceptions, upon contemplation of the unchangeable sky of a higher reality.

It is, as we have seen, precisely this withdrawal into the realm of abstraction which characterizes art at the transition from Antiquity to the Middle Ages.[5] Immediate sensory perception has lost its strength and joy. The overflowing richness of form in nature in all its tangible beauty and abundance, no longer moves the artist. The whole outer world, according to the language of the time, is a confusion in his senses, a deceitful illusion, a misty dream. Behind the fleeting world of nature, art perceives the large regular contours in an unchangeable, supernatural hierarchy of forces and ideas, of substances and beings, and attempts to capture this eternal order by new abstract means of expression, by a system of fixed formulas of types and of compositions. Such a stereotype has, however, a negative side, namely, schematization which, as we shall see, corresponds to a peculiar a priori

[5] For the much discussed late classical transcendentalism, the central factor of late classical art, see G. Rodenwaldt, *CAH*, xii, p. 563.

formation of concepts and a summary way of thinking both in the legislation and in the practical organization of the life of the period.

A striking parallel to that which occurs in art is the remarkable new reinterpretation and revaluation of the whole classical mythology during the Roman Empire. The god and the hero are thought of in the abstract: instead of the mythical beings in their concrete situations, one searches for the internal truth, the hidden meaning behind the figure and its action. Divinity, myth, and legend lose their substance, but receive a new content in allegory and symbol. The myth is a lie, we learn, but "a lie which depicts the truth." Like a shell the myth encloses this truth which is its new core and "interior."[6]

Everywhere there is the same negation of what is concrete, plastically delimitated and determined, the same turning towards simplifying concepts and symbolic absolutes. In an imperial triumph it is no longer the historical victor who is celebrated, the victor who conquered a specific enemy at a particular time and place; rather, the historical victor is elevated to the absolute victor, the *ubique victor*, the *victor omnium gentium*; his historical victory becomes the *victoria perpetua*—thus the emperor and his imperial victory are named on late antique coins and thus he is represented in triumphal art. On the Arch of Constantine, it is not only the representatives of the nations Constantine actually conquered who are laid at his feet, but representatives of the sum of Rome's enemies; and in a similar way the river gods depicted on the Arch no longer represent a specific geographical locality, but the totality of *orbis Romanus*.

Abstract man with eyes immersed in a transcendent world: is it not just this man whose own living self

[6] F. Cumont, *Recherches sur le symbolisme funéraire des Romains*, Paris, 1942, *passim*.

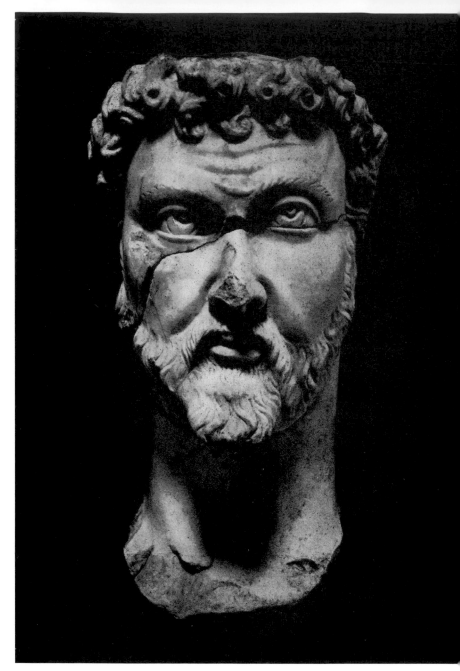

18. Portrait head, Ostia, v cent. A.D.

stands before us embodied in late antique portraits (for example, Fig. 18). In the great picture gallery of the Empire a change in the whole physiognomical typology takes place towards the end of the third century: a change that eloquently accompanies the change in mentality mentioned above. The eye is now directed towards a new goal: it looks past the things surrounding man, through time and space—indeed, through the whole tangible reality—and rests upon a point at an endless distance (compare Figs. 61 and 66). "The eye is the mirror of the soul"—and the eye we here describe has been pointed out by students of antique portraiture as the most profound physiognomical characteristic of the human image during Late Antiquity: this distant glance which gives such a distinctive expression not only to the artistic portrait but also to man himself as we see him in the spiritual life and behind the whole state and civic life of the Dominate. It looks through our elusive, changing, discordant, physical world and immerses itself in the higher absolutes, the unchangeable symmetry, in the realm of eternity.

THE GREAT CRISIS AND
ITS SOLUTION
UNDER DIOCLETIAN

I. THE REFORMS OF DIOCLETIAN

DIOCLETIAN

DIOCLETIANUS—in private life called Diocles—began his reign by administering justice in his own person: with his own hand he executed the man considered guilty of murdering the ruling emperor in the East, Numerian. On the high tribunal, before the eyes of the assembled army, he stabbed Aper, the Commander of the Praetorian Guard. Equally dramatic was his departure from the summit of power. Upon the high tribunal, again before the eyes of the assembled army, he took the purple from his shoulders and threw it about the new Caesar whom he had chosen; Diocletian was once again Diocles. The whole rule of Diocletian is characteristically framed by these two acts of state. A brief description of them may, therefore, serve as an introduction to this study of Diocletian's reforms.

In A.D. 284, the Roman armies under Emperor Numerian were marching home from a Persian campaign. The Emperor, suffering from an eye infection, was carried in a sedan-chair which concealed him from sight. He was accompanied by his father-in-law, Aper, prefect of the Praetorian Guard. One day a macabre stench emanated from the royal sedan-chair, and soon the whole army knew that it was occupied by a corpse. "Immediately all fell upon Aper who could no longer hide his treachery, and they dragged him before the banners in front of the high command in the camp. The soldiers flocked together to form a great military gathering and erected a tribunal. When the question was posed as to who, with greatest right, was to be Numerian's avenger and a good ruler of the Roman Empire, all in heaven-sent accord (*divino consensu*) conferred the title of Augustus upon Diocletian, who, it was said, had already received a portent of his future imperium. This man now ascended the tribunal and was hailed Augustus. When asked how Numerian had been murdered, Diocletian pointed with his drawn sword to Aper, the Praetorian Prefect, and driving it through him said: "This is Numerian's murderer."[1]

At the imperial twenty-year jubilee in Rome, A.D. 303, Diocletian, with his extraordinary will power, had persuaded Maximian, his co-Emperor in the West, to swear by Jupiter Capitolinus that he would abdicate simultaneously with Diocletian, in accordance with the new order of succession. Thus on the very same and historic day, but with a continent between them, the eastern and the western Emperors abdicated to be succeeded by the two Caesars, each in his own part of the Empire, in this way solemnly affirming the collegiate principle of the four-man rule of the Empire which sustained the whole new order of state. The abdication of Diocletian is described by Lactantius. On May 1, 305, we read, the eastern armies, together with representatives from the whole imperial army, are deployed upon a hill near Diocletian's residence, Nicomedia in Asia Minor, on the exact spot where Diocletian had bestowed the purple upon his eastern co-Emperor, Galerius. Upon this hill was erected a column crowned by a statue of Jupiter, the god-protector of Diocletian's whole order of state. Diocletian ascends the tribunal. In tears he addresses the army: his work is completed, he wishes to relinquish his power. "And so, suddenly, he proclaims Severus and Maximinus Daza the new Caesars" alongside of the two older Caesars who are now promoted to Augusti. "He divests himself of the purple and places it around the shoulders of Maximinus Daza. *Et Diocles iterum factus est.* The abdicated Emperor now steps down from the tribunal. He drives

[1] *Script. hist. aug., Vita Car., Carin. et Num.,* 12-15.

through the city in a simple gallic carriage, he travels far away and withdraws to the land of his birth."[2]

A rather brutal rectitude and an almost pathetic sense of duty speak to us in these contrasting but equally revealing scenes. The two acts, upon assuming and upon relinquishing power, sharply profile the reign of Diocletian; they show the active man's imprint upon events, the energetic intervention in the course of history—in short, the personality which creates history. This picture becomes clearer when one studies the rule of Diocletian and the governmental acts upon which the new state developed. As far as I can see, the basic features of the picture do not change if one sees in Diocletian, as did earlier historians, the great systematizer who pressed a ready-made governmental system upon the Empire, or if one sees him as William Seston does in his great work on Diocletian,[3] and in our opinion rightly, as the vigorous man of action who reacted to the challenge of events with strong measures and defensive efforts which only gradually took the form of a new system of government.

Under this energetic regime which took without mercy the full consequences demanded by the situation and followed every line of thought to the very end, tendencies come into view which had long been latent in both the spiritual and material life of the time.

THE GREAT CRISIS

In the second half of the third century the Roman Empire went through a shattering crisis which accelerated the transition from Principate to Dominate. Terrible wars, both internal and external, threw the Empire into a chaos in which all remnants of the traditional civic and social order became more or less completely dissolved. It

---

[2] Lactantius, *De mort. pers.*, I, 19.
[3] Above, p. 7, note 10.

is necessary in this connection to sketch briefly the *disintegrated* Roman Empire which forms the background for Diocletian's appearance and the founding of the new tetrarchic form of government.

During the second half of the third century all the borders of the Empire were invaded: along the northern frontiers invasions of Franks, Alamanni, Vandals, Goths, Sarmatians; from the Black Sea incursions of Gothic vikings into the Mediterranean; pressure of the Sassanian Persians in the east; invasions of Blemmyes, Libyans, and Mauretanians in the south. At the same time incessant murder of the emperors and usurpation of power took place within the Empire; the separate provinces severed ties and became organized against one another under their provincial armies and usurpers; constant civil war broke up the old Empire. Trebellius Pollio, though with the aid of imagination, tells of thirty usurpers (*tyranni triginta*) who, during the reign of Emperor Gallienus, "from all parts of the realm stormed towards the Empire."[4] Everywhere power was in the possession of the local army which proclaimed its leaders emperors. The traditional connections between the provinces were dissolved and the unity of the Empire was shattered. We find ourselves in a strangely *de-composed* Empire, with the provinces in mutual conflict.[5]

Chaos on the economic front accompanied this confusing state of affairs. Devaluation of money, resulting from the diminution of the amount of precious metal in the coin, led to inflation and violently fluctuating prices. There was a constant increase in taxes to maintain the standing armies; there were continual requisitions of provisions, especially of farm products, for armies on the move. Financial and monetary difficulties

[4] *Script. hist. aug., Tyranni Triginta,* 1.
[5] Oertel, *op.cit.,* pp. 260 ff.

The Reforms of Diocletian

forced the state to take what it needed in kind instead of the unreliable, increasingly devaluated money brought in by normal taxation.

All this, naturally, was first of all felt by the propertied classes, who groaned under the burden of taxes, military requisitions, intolerable *munera* (pp. 4 ff.). It was not unusual for municipal officials to surrender their whole fortune in order to free themselves from the forced duties it entailed. At the same time we hear of flights from homesteads and of the refusal to work, a form of strike.[6] The literary sources give a vivid glimpse into a period of terror, murder, and confiscations. Also to be taken into consideration in this connection was the hostility of the military proletariat of the provinces, who were then in power, to the bourgeois economic and social order—indeed, against the whole culture which it represented.[7] The traditional forms in the world of art and culture were disintegrating—we will see this point again (pp. 87 ff.; 111 ff.). In religion a symbiosis of the most divergent beliefs was established simultaneously with the penetration and transformation of the traditional Greco-Roman Olympus by an invasion of influences from the provinces, especially by Eastern religions and philosophies. Unrest and alarm was everywhere. Nothing was secure.

In this chaotic situation Diocletian made his appearance upon the stage of world history. He was the new Jupiter on earth who would master chaos and fling the rebelling giants to the ground; it was in this aspect that Diocletian was celebrated by panegyrists and artists (p. 79). The divided Empire was again united, a confused humanity rearranged itself, activities were again gathered up and distributed in a community-like order. But this

[6] *Ibid.*, pp. 265 ff.
[7] M. Rostovtzeff, *The Social and Economic History of the Roman Empire*, Oxford, 1941, pp. 376 ff.

order was now contained within a system of absolutes, the Dominate. The transformation, outlined above, of the Principate's forms of life—a transformation which actually had begun in the early part of the second century—was only accomplished with the reforms of Diocletian after the great crisis in the second half of the third century.

THE TETRARCHIC STATE SYSTEM

During the third century A.D., the century of the soldier-emperors, it had become accepted practice for armies to proclaim the emperors; the senate with its investiture could only confirm the fact. In the divided Empire it was not sufficient, however, that only a single provincial army supported the election of an emperor, as, after the death of Numerian (pp. 37 f.), the eastern armies were responsible for the election of Diocletian. After the murder of Emperor Carinus, Numerian's father, Diocletian also became commander of the western armies and took up the legitimate position as universal ruler of the Roman Empire (A.D. 285). One would expect the Emperor at this point to repay his debt with a declaration of loyalty to the imperial army; Diocletian's first governmental declaration, on the contrary, was a proclamation of his sovereignty. All the mints of the Empire now struck coins which did not, as had been the custom, carry legends such as *fides militum* or *concordia militum*, but rather *Jupiter conservator augusti*, invoking for the Emperor a divine protection that sanctified his leadership. In his dealings with the senate he was just as sovereign as in his relationship with the army. As far as one can judge from the numismatic material, he did not find it necessary to visit Rome in order to receive the investiture of the senate;[8] at the beginning of 286 he was in Nicomedia in Asia Minor, his permanent residence.

With divine sovereignty Diocletian now built up the new governmental system which secured the integrity of the Roman Empire. The separate parts in the structure of this new system were originally created—according to Seston—as necessary security measures in a given historical situation and only gradually did they grow together into a logical structural whole. Thus when, in 285/86, Diocletian appointed Maximian co-ruler and adopted him as *filius augusti*, with the title of *nobilissimus caesar*, it was mainly in order to gain a loyal and effective ally in the western provinces of the Empire, while he himself, watched over the eastern; Maximian was to secure the western border against the threatening pressure from invasions by Frankish, Germanic, and other barbaric tribes, and at the same time pacify the peasant insurrection in Gallia, the Bagaudae rebellion. When in 286 Diocletian's protégé, Carausius, usurped imperial power in Britannia and proclaimed himself emperor, Maximian could not have a rank lower than the usurper-augustus he was to combat; Maximian, therefore, was called upon to participate in the governing of the Empire and was elevated to Augustus.[9] With this Diarchy—with one Augustus in the East and one in the West—the process of division was introduced which led into the Tetrarchy's "symmetric" state order, with four ruling emperors.

Maximian's expedition against Carausius failed and the unity of the Roman Empire was endangered. Diocletian

[8] Seston, pp. 54, 205 ff. The Senate became important to Diocletian as an expression of *consensus omnium*, that is, the acceptance of his government by the whole population of the Empire. In this sense the *Genius Senatus* is represented, for example, on the monument erected by Diocletian on the Forum Romanum (see below, p. 67, Fig. 22).

[9] Seston, pp. 59 ff., 76.

reacted again as in 285/86: in 293 he elevated Costantius Chlorus to Caesar at the side of Maximian. He was to continue the fight against the warring usurper in Britannia while Maximian guarded the Rhine border.[10] When, a short time later, Diocletian elevated Galerius to Caesar at his own side, it was again under the pressure of the historical situation.[11] As in the West, an equal danger now threatened in the East: it was in the years 290/93 that the Sassanian Empire attempted to recover the Persian lands from Rome. Galerius became Caesar in 293, three months later than Constantius.[12]

Thereby the tetrarchic Empire was completely constituted. The whole Empire was now ruled according to a constitutional system which secured it from outside attack and prevented usurpations within. There was one Augustus in the East and one in the West, and each of them had a Caesar at his side. At the death of an Augustus, the Caesar beside him promptly took his place. The Empire was thus armed against any aggression, from whatever side and against whatever part of the realm it might be directed. The legitimate Empire was also secured within against murder of the emperor and usurpation. The fundamental principle of the whole structure was found in the continually proclaimed imperial *concordia*, on which was based the delegation of power, the balance, the imperturbable suprapersonal *symmetry* of the Tetrarchy. "L'institution impériale reçut pour couronnement un édifice imprévu aux lignes symétriques."[13]

Closely linked with the new system of government was a form of succession that surely is unique in monarchical history and, at the same time, extremely characteristic of the symmetrical structure of the Tetrarchy. At the termination of a given period of reign, which perhaps

[10] Seston, pp. 88 f. [11] Seston, pp. 89 f.
[12] Seston, p. 94. [13] Seston, p. 100.

was intended to be twenty years, both Augusti were required to abdicate on the same day, and simultaneously both Caesars advanced to Augusti while two new Caesars were advanced to assist them. To prevent undue influence upon the new Tetrarchy from the abdicated *seniores augusti*, they were required to remove themselves from the imperial residences and withdraw to retirement palaces in the provinces. Nor were these mechanics of succession, though so well adapted to the governmental system of the tetrarchic state, the result of a system. They had grown out of the historical situation in order to avoid usurpations and rivalries over the throne—as a necessity, in consequence of life itself.

Thus the emperors' periods of reign, their succession and abdication, their jubilees, etc., occurred in regular cadence, or at least were planned to do so according to the system. The biographical data in the reign of the emperors were forced into a depersonalized, rhythmic succession. Thus, for example, after some years had passed, the anniversary of the ascension to the throne of the two Caesars, their *dies imperii*, was celebrated on the same day and likewise the place of their investiture—again contrary to the actual fact—became one and the same. "Pour répondre au gout de la symétrie."[14] The *dies imperii* of the one emperor, the place of his investiture, the anniversary of his jubilee, and the year of his abdication are assumed by the other, just as the one emperor's portrait is substituted for the other's on coins (p. 121). When, for example, Diocletian in November 303 celebrated his *vicennalia* in the old capital of the Empire, Maximian was also the hero of the day, and simultaneously both of the Caesars celebrated their *decennalia*. The event was commemorated with a monument erected behind the Rostra at Forum Romanum, a monument which

---

[14] Seston, p. 94.

can be reconstructed on the basis of the surviving fragments and a rendering of it on a relief on the Arch of Constantine.[15] It consisted of five huge columns crowned by statues: at the center Jupiter and, symmetrically grouped around him, the four emperors, all of them of exactly the same type.

A system of "double-principate"[16] was also known to the earlier Empire, for example, the co-rule of Marcus Aurelius and Lucius Verus. But it was not until the Tetrarchy that the conception of a twin-Empire was developed where the two Augusti appeared as complete equals and alike—cast from the same mold, so to speak. In Mamertinus' speech in honor of Maximian on his "birthday" in A.D. 291, we meet for the first time this conception of the emperors' ideal similarity. At the pinnacle of the Roman Empire stood a twin-god, *numen geminatum*.[17] The similarity of the emperors is evident in their whole being, their physical exterior, even their age.[18] "The immortal gods cannot divide their benefactions between you; that which is given to one of you, belongs to you both."[19] Coin portraits proclaim with equal emphasis the *similitudo* of the emperors; as said above, this assimilation was carried so far as to enable one emperor portrait to be substituted for another and thus to be considered current under the four different imperial names.[20] The emperors are portrayed alike also in mon-

[15] L'Orange, "Ein tetrarchisches Ehrendenkmal auf dem Forum Romanum," *Mitteilungen des Deutschen Archäeolog. Instituts, Röm. Abt.*, 53, 1938, pp. 1 ff. H. Kähler, *Das Fünfsäulendenkmal für die Tetrarchen auf dem Forum Romanum*, Cologne, 1964, pp. 5 ff.

[16] E. Kornemann, *Doppelprinzipat . . . im Imperium Romanum*, Leipzig, 1930.

[17] E. Galletier, *Panégyriques Latins I, Mamertini genethl. Max.*, 11.

[18] *Ibid.*, 7.

[19] *Ibid.*

[20] J. Maurice, *Numismatique Constantinienne*, 1, Paris, 1911, pp. 4 f. L'Orange, *Studien*, pp. 101 f.

umental sculpture (pp. 121 ff.), for example, in the well-
known porphyry groups in Venice and in the Vatican
(Figs. 19-21).[21] One and all are represented in high relief, almost as sculpture in the round projecting from
porphyry columns and arranged in pairs. Each pair is of
equal height, with the same dress and weapon, the same
decorations and insignias, the same posture and gesture,
and joined in the same expressive embrace—the image of
their *concordia*. The perfect *similitudo* affects also the
physiognomical type, the facial features, and above all
the expressions—this is best seen in the Vatican groups
where each pair represents a more or less mechanical
duplication of the same figure. Also in the aforemen-
tioned tetrarchic monument at Forum Romanum and in
the tetrarch-group on a relief on the Arch of Galerius in
Thessalonika (Fig. 40) is the *similitudo* of the emperors
articulated in their type, dress, gesture, and entire appearance.

This *similitudo* that we meet in the portraits of emperors by panegyrists, in coin portraits, and in monumental sculpture, has its own explanation, which gives an
important glimpse into the theocratical ideas of the Dominate. The key to the understanding of it lies in the seemingly inconsequential fact that both Augusti celebrate
their "birthday" on the same day: this birthday, *gemini
natales*, is actually not their proper and personal birthday,
but their joint divine birthday, calculated from the day
in 287 when the two Augusti adopted the names Jovius
and Herculius, after their fathers Jupiter and Hercules.[22]
On this common origin the *similitudo* of the emperors
is founded. The identical emperor type with its divine

[21] R. Delbrück, *Antike Porphyrwerke*, Berlin, 1932, pp. 84 f., pls.
31-34; pp. 91 f., pls. 35-37. L'Orange, *Studien*, pp. 16 ff., figs. 32-35.

[22] Seston, pp. 211 ff. E. Galletier, *op.cit.*, 1, *Mamertini paneg. Max.*,
10 ff. Compare *Mamertini genethl. Max.*, 2.

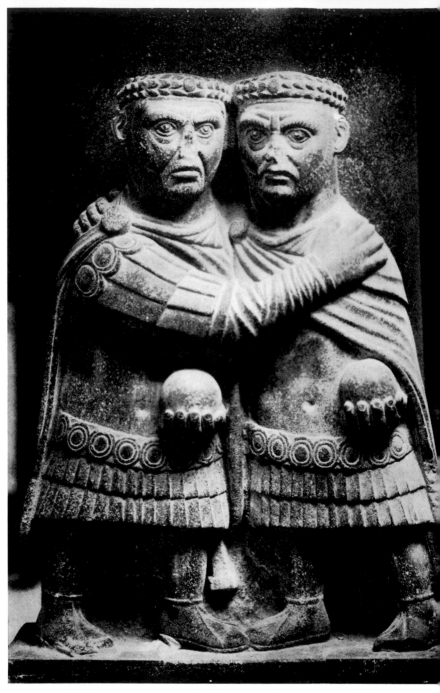

19. Porphyry group of the Tetrarchy, the two Augusti, Vatican

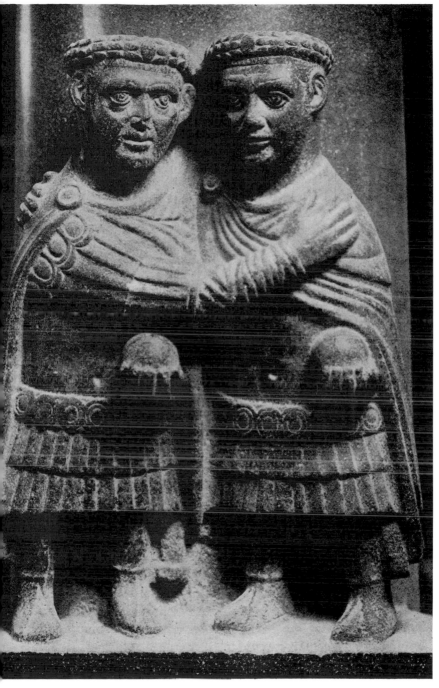

20. Porphyry group of the Tetrarchy, the two Caesars, Vatican

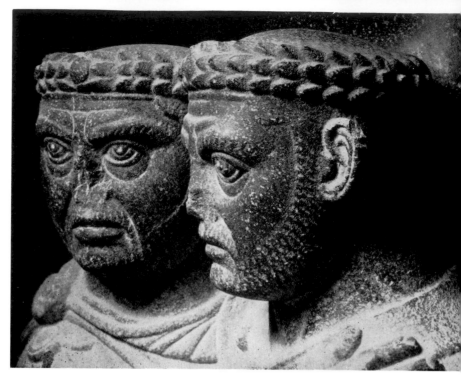

21. Detail of porphyry group of Fig. 19

origin replaces the personal individuality, just as the divine birthday replaces the personal *dies natalis*. The *similitudo* in the portraying of the emperors is thus of the same nature as that in the portrayal of saints; a "sacred type," τύπος ἱερός (pp. 121 ff.) permeates all individual characteristics. It is toward this manifestation of the divine in the emperors and not toward their individual personality that the eye of Late Antiquity is directed, it seeks the eternal God-Emperor which undoubtedly was seen in the image of Diocletian. The individual personality is replaced by the type. The imperial *concordia* itself, the basis of the tetrarchic government, is built upon this *similitudo* of the emperors: *hac ipsa vestri similitudine magis magisque concordes.*[23]

[23] *Mamertini paneg. Max.*, 9.

The *concordia* of the emperors expressed itself in the complete mutual equality of the two Augusti and of the two Caesars. In the court ceremonial the two Augusti stood as divine twins, side by side, so that the adoring subjects had to lay aside the traditional form of worship directed toward the single God-Emperor; instead, a new ceremony of worship was established with double adoration (*duplicatum pietatis officium*).[24] At gatherings the emperors always appeared together. During their discussions they clasped hands.[25] They drove in the same carriage and the onlookers shouted with joy as it passed, they pointed and exclaimed: *Vides Diocletianum? Maximianum vides? Ambo sunt, pariter sunt. Quam iunctim sedent! Quam concorditer colloquuntur.*[26] As in the emperors' *similitudo*, a higher stability and regularity, a divine order, was manifest also in their *concordia*. "What century has ever seen a like *concordia* at the summit of power? Which brothers, what twins respect one another's equal rights to undivided property as You Your equal right to the Roman Empire? Through all this is revealed that though other human souls be worldly and transient, Yours are celestial and eternal (*caelestes et sempiternes*)."[27] It is therefore, Heaven which makes itself known in the mutual *similitudo* and *concordia* of the emperors, in the whole imperturbable symmetry of the tetrarchic Empire. The very dividing of the Empire into four quarters is derived from Heaven. In this godly number resides all the highest strength and joy (*Isto numinis vestro numero summa omnia nituntur et gaudent*). The panegyrist speaking these words to Constantius Chlorus, praises the anchoring of the whole universe in the cosmic number four—there are four elements, four seasons, four corners

---

[24] *Mamertini genethl. Max.*, 11. [25] *Ibid.*, 12.
[26] *Ibid.*, 11. [27] *Ibid.*, 6.

of the earth, four horses in the quadriga of the sun, four celestial lights, etc.[28]

The description of the "advent" of Diocletian and Maximian to Italy and their meeting in Mediolanum in the winter of 290-91,[29] gives an idea of what conceptions were connected with the Emperors as *dei praesentes*. The winter transforms itself into spring; the approach of the Emperors gleams over the peaks of the Alps, all Italy shines in a clearer light; not only people but also herds of animals, leaving their forests and distant pastures, swarm forth where the Emperors pass. The entire population celebrates, flames adorn all altars, wine and animals are sacrificed, there is the fragrance of incense from the altars; everywhere the people rejoice, everywhere dance and applause. "Hymns of praise and thanksgiving to the immortal Gods were sung, Jupiter was invoked at close range, not as he appeared in the ordinary conception but as visible and physically present (*conspicuus et praesens Jupiter*); Hercules was worshiped, not as a stranger, but in the very person of the Emperor."[30] The divine Empire permeates nature and the elements. "Wherever You are, even when You have retired into one and the same Palace, everywhere Your divinity is present, the whole earth and all the seas are filled with You."[31]

The emperors are, therefore, gods elevated above the Empire they govern. "Your immortal soul is greater than any power, any fortune, yes, even than the Empire"— *ipso est maior imperio*.[32] Their power is absolute, their right to form the world, set free and bind humanity, is unlimited. Independent of the senate and the army, Jovius Diocletianus can himself create emperors, i.e., appoint his co-emperors and successors who—created by him—

[28] E. Galletier, *op.cit.*, IV, *Incerti paneg. Constantio Caesari*, 4.
[29] *Mamertini genethl. Max.*, 6.   [30] *Ibid.*, 10.
[31] *Ibid.*, 14.   [32] *Ibid.*, 6; cf. 2.

are gods. The emperors are, as it is said in an inscription, "born of God and themselves creators of Gods."[33] In reality it is Jupiter himself, the *summus pater*[34] of all the emperors, who is present at the investiture and who adopts as a son the new Augustus or the new Caesar. The titles of Jovius and Herculius given to the Caesars of 293 and 305 on the day of their nomination were a justification of the choice; it is Jupiter himself who had chosen.[35]

The tetrarchic state rested thus, firmly and immovably, in the eternal world order. In the constitution and the administration of the state, in financial reforms, economic and social stabilization measures, in war and peace, cultural and religious politics—everywhere the Jupiter-Empire of Diocletian was present as the organizing force. The reforms carried out in all sectors of life introduced one single order willed by the gods. As Jovii and Herculei, the emperors belonged to a higher world "où ils ont trouvé une sorte d'harmonie préétablie qu'aucun d'eaux ne pouvait contester ou changer" (W. Seston). The great regularity and lawfulness of this higher and eternal world now, with the reform work of Diocletian, descended into our temporal reality, and the confusing multitude of obstinate and unruly natural forms were aligned and arranged according to the strict lines of a transcendent order and symmetry.

Let us see how the Tetrarchy organized this new order in some of the central spheres in the life of the state and the individual.

THE TETRARCHIC STATE ADMINISTRATION

A characteristic feature of the administrative reform was the splitting up of the large and organic provincial

---

[33] Seston, p. 218.   [34] Seston, pp. 217 ff.   [35] Seston, p. 231.

territories into smaller, more uniform and mutually equal parts, about one hundred in number, which were then grouped into twelve larger administrative units (*dioeceses*). Italy and Egypt also, in spite of having had their special, historically qualified status, were regulated according to the general scheme with partitioning into small provinces aggregated into dioceses.[36] In accordance with the uniform nature of the new small provinces, all the provincial governors had the same title: that of judge (*judex*). At the head of each diocese were the *vicarii* for the four Praetorian Prefects, while the prefects themselves represented the highest division of the Empire, the four prefectures corresponding to the divine tetrarchical order itself. In the governing of all these administrative units—province, diocese, prefecture—a vertical dividing line was drawn (except where defense installations were threatened with imminent danger) between the civil and the military administration. *Judices* and *vicarii*, later also the prefects, were in principle to be civil servants only. Beside them were the military commanders (*duces*).

In this checkered carving-up of the territories into new, equal, and uniform administrative units, arranged in three levels, a scheme of division was employed which was characteristic of the tetrarchical system. Here is a construction that can be compared to composition according to a geometrical coordinate system in contemporary art and architecture (pp. 71 f., Fig. 23). The complex and composite were not resolved into their natural components, but were divided more mathematically and appeared, after this division, as regular and equal parts.

[36] Compare the way in which Diocletian made the fortification of the *limes* uniform along all of the borders; from the Sahara to the Syrian desert, from the Rhine to the coast of Britannia, there is now a oneness as never before in the *castra* and all the defenses of the *limes* (Seston, p. 297).

The Reforms of Diocletian

Still, this administrative geometry, no less than the tetrarchic system, was not part of a predetermined plan
but the result of historical circumstances. Both the dividing up of the provinces and the separation of the civil
and military administration were intended to split the
concentration of power and thereby prevent usurpation—
the latent danger ever-present in the enormous Empire.
Simultaneously, Diocletian completed the total inte-
gration of the municipalities into the state whereby they
lost the last remnants of an organic life of their own. As
we have seen, the various civic functions in the cities
gradually became obligatory duties or services, which
were laid upon the wealthy citizens, and were increasingly organized in the interests of the state and less in
that of the municipalities. The magistrates of the municipalities, their public organizations, even individuals from
the propertied classes, were now placed under the authority of the provincial governors, while the latter in turn
were controlled by the imperial central administration
through its vicars. In this way the central administration,
surmounting a hierarchy of functionaries whose authority
increased as they approached the pyramid's peak, mag-
netically drew all activities in toward itself: toward the
emperor in his *consistorium*.[37]

THE TAX REFORM OF DIOCLETIAN

During the earlier Empire the collection of state revenues, such as taxes and custom duties, were farmed out
to private citizens (*publicani*), who could become rich
in this business. Later city officials and council members
were appointed as collectors of these state revenues. During the third century, as we have seen, an increasingly
hard policy of taxation made these collectors, who rep-

[37] Seston, pp. 343 ff.

resented the wealthy citizens, personally liable for the full return of the collection.

Diocletian now introduced a new standard of value which made possible a thorough and systematic utilization of all the existing resources of value.[38] The peculiar late antique tax, called *capitatio* (head tax), created by Diocletian, instituted a new unit (*caput*) beside the traditional *iugum*, as a basis for taxation. A "head" or "person" tax (*caput*) was added to the property tax. While the traditional unit of assessment (*iugum*) was used only for land, the Diocletian *caput*, did not, as one would think, apply only to people but also to animals and land. The same word, *capitatio*, was used without differentiation for the tax to be paid for the people who work the soil and the tax levied on the soil itself and the animals it nourishes. As a fiscal quantity the *iugum* and the *caput* are equivalent even though the objects of taxation, people and land, are fundamentally different. Thus, the tax register in some districts shows that *capita* and *iuga* were added together, as both were united under the term ζυγοκέφαλα.[39]

Piganiol has assumed—and Seston follows him—that this assessment of both humans and land in *capita*, was advanced as a practical solution inspired by the historical circumstances at the time when Diocletian intervened in the chaotic conditions, which also in the fiscal area characterized the period of dissolution in the second half of the third century. Inflation increasingly necessitated the demand that taxes be collected in kind, particularly grain,

---

[38] We recall the harsh words of Lactantius about what he calls the *avaritia* of Diocletian, which burdens the people with such new taxes as the farmers cannot bear and they are forced to abandon the soil: *ut enormitate indictionum consumptis viribus colonorum desererentur agri* (*De mort. pers.*, 7).

[39] Seston, p. 275. H. Bott, *Die Grundzüge der Diokletian. Steuerverfassung*, Darmstadt, 1928, pp. 40 ff.

but also raw material and manufactured goods. Everywhere armies were on the march and everywhere there were impending requisitions of the supplies that were to insure the army's *annona*, their store of the yearly corn supply. Diocletian's *capitatio* seems to have raised the summary taxation practiced by these military requisitions to a permanent institution. By a summary estimate of the cultivated land, cattle, and the number of working "heads" on an estate, one could evaluate its wealth and fix the size of the requisition. With the systematic utilization of all resources it became natural to use a standard of measure that could be applied to everything; a unit of measure was settled upon that represented the amount of agricultural produce equal to a *caput*, i.e., the needs of a single farm-worker.[40] Thus arose an oversimplified and generalized system, without adjustment to the changes in economic life and the shifts in the social structures in the different provinces.[41] Such a system of taxation, which lumped together the land and its inhabitants, at the same time favored the general tendency to bind the farmer and tenant farmer to his native soil.

At the beginning of his reign Diocletian has sought an immediate result by his reforms and was content for the time being with summary evaluations in order to raise the *annona*. In the tax reform of 297, estates were counted, land, animals, and humans accurately assessed, and the equivalent apportionment of *capita* was set, in accordance with the divine providence of the emperor. "Nos empereurs très prévoyants, Dioclétien, etc. . . . ont décidé . . . de publier un règlement salutaire (τύπον σωτήριον), auquel on doit se conformer pour fixer les impôts. Quelle charge a été imposée à chaque aroure, d'après la qualité de la terre, e quelle charge à chaque

<hr/>

[40] A. Piganiol, *RHist*, 1935, p. 1. Cf. Seston, pp. 274 ff.
[41] Kornemann, *Weltgeschichte*, p. 259.

tête de paysan, et depuis quel âge jusqu'à quel âge, il
est loisible à tous de la connaître . . . Après avoir été
gratifiés de si grands bienfaits, que les provinciaux
s'empressent de payer leurs impôts très promptement,
conformément aux règles posées par la décision divine,
et qu'ils n'attendent pas l'intervention des compulsores."[42]

Of special importance from our point of view is the
fact that the *capitatio* of Diocletian made persons and
things equivalent so that for the purpose of taxation they
could be added as ζυγοκέφαλα. A farmer paid for himself or his worker the same quantity of agricultural produce or the equivalent in goods that he pays for a determined area of his estate or a certain number of heads of
his cattle. "Une côte fiscale est crée dans l'abstrait, le
caput, et dans ce moule tout sera jeté, les hommes et la
terre, et les animaux qui vivent de la terre."[43] Here
again, we meet the peculiar attitude of Late Antiquity,
which is not concerned with individuality and the nature
of things but applies to everything one and the same
common denominator, reduces forms to homogeneous
units, and marshals them in unending rows. One may
compare with this what we saw in the *spolia* architecture
of Late Antiquity, where building elements of widely
different function and form were made equal within the
totality of the structure and made to function in one and
the same way.

THE PRICE LAW

Diocletian's endeavors to stabilize the currency was an
attempt, continuing that of the Emperor Aurelian, to
conquer the perilous inflation that had arisen during
periods of crisis in the third century when a state of

[42] A. Piganiol's translation, *op.cit.*, p. 1 (repeated Seston, p. 283), of
the imperial decree dispatched by the prefect of Egypt.
[43] Seston, pp. 281, 288.

The Reforms of Diocletian

emergency led, as it had at earlier periods of the Roman Empire, to the minting of debased coins. Like Aurelian, he resumed the minting of full-value gold and silver coins, *aureus* to 1/60 pound, *argenteus* to 1/96 pound, as under Nero. The copper coinage (*follis, radiatus* and *denarius communis*), was, however, as before, not of full-value copper. The over-evaluation of the copper coins in comparison to the gold and silver was the cause of disturbances in the new monetary system. *"Valutarische Gewaltstreiche,"* to use Regling's phrase, in the end completely destroyed confidence in Diocletian's financial system and led to an increasing rise of costs in the Empire.[44] To stabilize prices, Diocletian intervened with his famous price law in A.D. 301. The law affixed a maximum tariff, which regulated all prices for goods, wages, and salaries on the basis of the *denarius* as the smallest monetary unit, the value of which was put at 1/50,000 pound gold.[45] In the preface to the price list a fundamental explanation for the establishment of such a maximum tariff is given: this encroachment upon the economic life, we read, is based on an eternal, god-willed judicial order, which was violated by the individual desire for profit. We relate here the main points contained in this preface.

Mention is made of "the furious avarice which, with no thought for mankind (*sine respectu generis humani*), hastens to its own gain and increases its property at a tempo which does not take into account years or months

[44] K. Regling, "Münzkunde" in Gercke-Norden, *Einleitung in die Altertumswissenschaft*, II, 2 (ed. 4), pp. 28 ff. Kornemann, *Weltgeschichte*, p. 263.
[45] Th. Mommsen-H. Blümner, *Edictum Diocletiani de pretiis rerum venalium*, Berlin, 1893. The original text is accompanied by an English translation by Elsa Graser, "The Edict of Diocletian" in Tenney Frank, *Economic Survey of Ancient Rome*, v, pp. 307 ff., Baltimore, 1940. Graser's publication of the tariff has also included fragments of inscriptions which came to light after the Mommsen-Blümner publication.

or days, but only hours and even minutes." The "furious avarice" and "untameable greed" (*avaritia, cupido furoris indomiti*) of the individual are in conflict with the "general welfare" (*fortunae communes; communis necessitudo*), and makes many people "enemies both of the single individual and of the universal order" (*inimici singulis et universis rebus*). This "unbridled passion for gain" (*effrenata libido rapiendi*) is mitigated neither by abundant supplies nor by fruitful years. Above all this affects the army. With "the monstrous prices that human speech is incapable of describing . . . it follows that in a single purchase a soldier is deprived of his bonus and salary and that the contributions of the whole world to support the armies fall to the abominable profit of thieves so that our soldiers seem with their own hands to offer the hopes of their service and of their completed labors to the profiteers, with the result that those who plunder the nation constantly take in more than they can use themselves."

With all this taken into consideration, the edict states, it is necessary for the state to intervene. "We (the emperors)—who are the protectors of the human race—viewing this state of affairs, find ourselves called upon to intervene with the rule of justice, so that the long-hoped-for solution which mankind itself could not supply, might be brought about, through our foresight, for the betterment of all. . . . It is our pleasure therefore, that the prices listed in the summary appended be observed in the whole of our Empire. . . . For buyers and sellers who customarily travel to foreign ports and provinces, this universal decree should be a warning so that they too know that in the time of high prices there is no opportunity of exceeding the fixed maximum prices, for example by including the location of the place or transportation . . . and so that the justice of our decree forbidding those who transport merchandise to sell anywhere at higher prices, may be evident."

"Since fear has always been regarded as the most influential preceptor in the performance of duty, it is in accordance with our will that anyone who shall have resisted the regulation set forth in this statute, shall for his daring be subject to the death penalty. . . . To the same penalty, moreover, is he subject who in the desire to buy shall have conspired against the statute with the greed of the seller. Nor are they exempt from the same penalty who, although possessing the necessities of life and business, believe that to escape this regulation, they may withdraw them from the general market. . . . We, therefore, appeal to the loyalty of all our people that a law created for the public good may be observed with willing obedience and due fear of God (*cohortamur ergo omnium devotionem ut res constituta ex commodo publico benignis obsequiis debita religione teneatur*)."

The individual desire for profit, is thus placed in contrast to "the general welfare" (*fortunae communes*), which is based upon a "universal order" (*res universae*) surpassing the individual. The divine Empire which is the realization on earth of this higher order, sets up the dominion of righteousness (*arbitram justitiam*) against lust of gain and establishes by its providence the higher order that mankind itself is not able to set up, everything for the common good (*ad comune omnium temperamentum*). The price law is based immovably upon *res universae* and must be upheld with pious devotion and fear of God (*devotio* and *religio*); he who offends this law sins against the divine—and imperial—order of life and has forfeited his life.

How abstract and detached from the realities of life the Diocletian price law was, is evident in the fact that the established maximum tariff was inflexibly the same all over the Roman world (*totus orbis*), in all places and at all times, in retail and wholesale. Again the eye skips over the concrete and realistic, seeks beyond detail and differentiation to rest upon the grand lines of the *res universae*.

DIOCLETIAN'S CULTURAL AND RELIGIOUS POLICY

Diocletian considered himself a Roman and wished to renew the Roman state, Roman religion and morals, Roman customs and mores, Roman civilization. In place of *Sol Invictus* which, since Severan times and, to an even higher degree, after Aurelian, had occupied the central position in the religion of the Empire, there appears once again, as we have seen, the national-Roman Jupiter, lord of the Capitol, and Hercules, hero of the Palatine. Diocletian's special relationship with Jupiter (pp. 38 ff.) fills him with a genuinely Roman religiosity. His *pietas* is commemorated by his contemporaries. "How great is Your piety for the gods," says a panegyrist to the two Augusti. "You have showered them with altars and statues, with temples and offerings which You embellished with Your image and inscribed name, and which You made even more holy by the example You set by your own worship of the gods. Now, surely, men understand what power resides in the gods when they are worshiped so fervently by You."[46] The reward for this imperial piety is happiness for the whole Empire (*Felicitatem istam, optimi imperatores, pietate meruistis*).[47] This happiness won by the *pietas* of the emperors, is a new golden *saeculum* and everlasting peace. In an inscription from the year 291, Diocletian is commemorated as "founder of the eternal peace."[48]

[46] *Mamertini genethl. Max.*, 6. [47] *Ibid.*, 18; cf. 6.
[48] CIL, III, 5810.

Such a joy-bearing Jupiter religion was intended to unite all Romans, to promote unity in thought and feeling, and to consolidate the whole Empire.[49] With the Jupiter religion follows the ideal of Roman civilization: *disciplina legesque Romanae*. All of the inhabited world, in spite of ethnic differences, had to be made alike following the precepts of Roman discipline and law. Diocletian sought therefore, as far as possible, to widen the areas of influence of Roman law and to remove from the law of the Empire the infiltration of non-Roman, especially Greek elements.[50] Roman law became a main pillar in the romanization of the provinces. But the peculiar character of this law required Latin as the judicial language. Diocletian, therefore, sent Latin rhetors and grammarians to the Greek-speaking eastern provinces. Even in Egypt, which up to now had occupied a special position somewhat apart, Latin became the judicial language; and even upon coins the Greek inscriptions gave way to Latin. The Dominate did not concern itself with the natural, individual lives of the eastern population but sought to instill Latin as the administrative language in the whole of the Greek-speaking east. Again, this was a result of the general process of equalization and uniformity which Kornemann describes as Diocletian's "Drang nach Gleichmacherei, Vereinfachung, Mechanisierung."[51]

In the marriage laws of Diocletian we have a typical result of these endeavors towards romanization. The Emperor turned against the more lenient practice of the third century, which was consistent with the complex

---

[49] Kornemann, *Weltgeschichte*, pp. 248 ff.

[50] K. Stade, *Der Politiker Diokletian und die letzte grosse Christenverfolgung*, n.pl., 1926, pp. 68 ff.

[51] Kornemann, *Weltgeschichte*, pp. 270 f. Cf. R. Laqueur in *Probleme der Spätantike*, 1930, 4, pp. 1 ff. Stade, *op.cit.*, pp. 67 f.

situation in the world Empire, with a diversity of popular customs in this intimate domain of life. Laws were established for marriage contracts, and family marriage was forbidden even though such marriages had become increasingly common and were, moreover, ancient custom in many parts of the eastern provinces. The ordinance specifies in detail all blood relationships which could conceivably preclude marriage contracts—it was thus forbidden to marry one's great-grandmother. *Disciplina legesque Romanae* is constantly the directing and regulating principle.[52] "To our pious and religious disposition it seems that what in Roman law is prescribed as chaste and holy is especially admirable and should be preserved with eternal religious veneration" (*ea quae Romanis legibus caste sancteque sunt constituta venerabilia maxime videntur atque aeterna religione servanda*). In the face of violations of these laws "the discipline of our time urges us to interfere."[53] Here the battle was fought against everything felt to be dissolving the traditional Roman form of life and culture.

The uniformness of religious life in the spirit of the Jupiter religion led to persecution of self-willed religious societies. In the midst of a world of tolerant Sun- or Cosmic religiosity where Roman and Greek were mingled with and had absorbed diverse elements of the religions of Egypt, Syria, Asia Minor, and Persia, and where the Hellenistic-Oriental mystery worship, gnosis, philosophy, and astrology permeated the traditional forms of Roman worship, efforts emerged towards the end of the third century to unify and fortify the Roman world under a state church: efforts which were only fulfilled with the constitution of the Christian state. The world strove toward a *rapprochement* of state and church in a way unknown before in Antiquity, but to

[52] Stade, *op.cit.*, p. 82.   [53] *Ibid.*, p. 79.

which close parallels can be found in the contemporary Empire in the east, the Sassanian Persia.[54] Immediately before Diocletian, Aurelian had put the Syrian sun religion, in a Romanized form, at the center of the state cult. Diocletian "causes the Emperors' gods to become leaders" (βασιλέων θεοὺς ἡγεμόνας ποιούμενος)[55]—in other words, he founded a kind of celestial Jupiter monarchy. Above the chaotic, infinitely complex religious world of the third century with its amalgamation or symbiosis of a multitude of diversified religions, now arose a well-regulated Olympus with Jupiter upon the central peak; and, reflecting this celestial Olympus, the Jovian Empire on earth surmounts the State. Nothing must violate this symmetry.

Diocletian's persecution of foreign cults was, in the religious sphere, completely parallel to contemporary intervention in all sectors of economic and social life. In the Manichee-edict of March 31, 297, the Tetrarchy proceeded with the severest punishments against the religion of Mani: against the insane and wretched "who set new and unheard-of teachings up against the older religions" (*qui novellas et inauditas sectas veterioribus religionibus opponunt*). The leaders of this movement were to burn, "together with their abominable writings" (*cum abominandis scripturis*), and their sympathizers were to be executed. "For it is the greatest crime to oppose that which —determined and decided by the fathers—has its firm place and its sure course."[56]

This violent intervention against the followers of Mani preludes the Tetrarchy's persecution of the Christians, which was the most extensive and systematic ever carried out by the Roman Empire. In the year 298 the armistice

---

[54] Kornemann, *Weltgeschichte*, p. 241.
[55] Libanius, *Orationes*, 4, p. 331, ed. Förster.
[56] Stade, *op.cit.*, p. 160.

between the state and the Christian community was broken after having existed for nearly forty years.[57] The Christians had refused to sacrifice to the emperor: that is, had refused to give the obligatory proof of loyalty to the present Jupiter. The state reacted by removing all Christians from its service, in particular from the army. The first general edict against the Christians followed on February 23, 303. The Christian meeting houses were ordered destroyed and cult assemblies forbidden; the holy scriptures and liturgical books were to be surrendered and burned; all Christians were outlawed. A short time after the issuing of this edict a fire broke out in the imperial palace at Nicomedia and the blame was laid upon the Christians. This gave rise to another and more rigorous edict: the whole of the Christian clergy was to be imprisoned. "Everywhere countless numbers were locked up and in every place the prisons, which had been built long ago for murderers and grave-robbers, were filled with bishops, elders, and deacons, with readers and exorcists, so that there was no longer room left in the prisons for convicted criminals."[58] A third edict ordered that the imprisoned Christians should be forced to sacrifice and then set free. At last there came the sanguinary fourth edict which commanded all Christians—men, women, and children—to sacrifice or die. The greatest period of Christian martyrdom had begun.

The original and deepest motive for the persecutions is apparent, according to K. Stade,[59] from Galerius' later edict of tolerance. The emperors would "improve everything according to the old Roman laws and public discipline" (*iuxta leges veteres et publicam disciplinam Romanorum cuncta corrigere*), and "would see that the Christians . . . came to their senses again." The emperors'

[57] Seston, pp. 122 ff., 155. [58] Eusebius, *Hist. eccl.*, VIII, 6, 9.
[59] Stade, *op.cit.*, pp. 162 f.

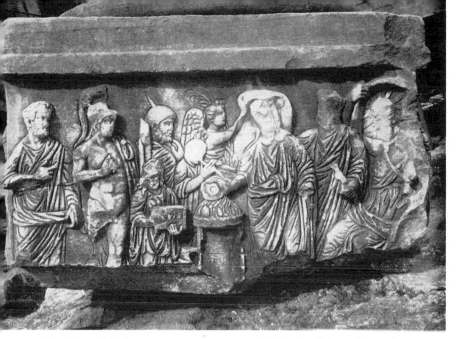

22. Tetrarchical emperor at the state sacrifice. Relief on base of column of honorary monument, Forum Romanum

intention with the persecutions was to have been "to lead all men's thoughts along the pious and right path of life" (πάντων τῶν ἀνθρώπων τὰς διανοίας πρὸς τὴν ὁσίαν καὶ ὀρθὴν τοῦ ζῆν ὁδὸν περιαγαγεῖν).[60] Only the Jupiter religion, however, could lead men along this path. In the year 303—contemporary with the persecution of the Christians—an imposing monument was erected at Forum Romanum which eloquently expresses this religion: the previously mentioned five-column monument dedicated on the occasion of the twentieth anniversary of the reign of the Augusti. The four Emperors, who are all identical, are grouped around the colossal Jupiter on the central column. On each of the column bases is depicted the sacrificing Emperor, an illustration of his *pietas* (Fig. 22). At the same time coins are struck showing Diocletian and Maximian at the state sacrifice,

[60] Eusebius, *op.cit.*, IX, I, 3.

accompanied by Felicitas, the personification of the happiness of the Empire, and surrounded by the symbols of peace, prosperity, and fertility. The legend reads: *felicitas temporum*. The *pietas* of the emperor guarantees the *felicitas* of the world.

Felicitatem istam, optimi imperatores, pietate meruistis. Thus, in accordance with the monument and the coins, the panegyrist addresses the Christian-persecuting emperors. There was, however, only one *pietas*: that which conformed with *disciplina legesque Romanae* and which resided in the perpetual order of Jupiter. We sense the contours of a compact tetrarchical state religion which was to unify and equalize the spiritual life of Rome.

II. TRANSFORMATIONS IN THE ART AND ARCHITECTURE OF THE DIOCLETIAN PERIOD

WE HAVE seen how the traditional forms of organization, both in the life of the state and of the individual, changed with the transition from Principate to Dominate. The new pattern is most clearly outlined in the Diocletian state. Let us sum up the main points of the transformation as we have described it in our preceding study.

The free and organic grouping of individuals and institutions was replaced by a mechanical coordination of the elements, by row formations and symmetry, everything was aligned according to the strict ordinates of a higher axial system, an order imposed from above. There is no eye for the individual, no feeling for the differentiations of an organically developing nature, no appreciation of detail and variety, but a peculiarly distant glance following the abstract lines of the inner unity of things and seeking fixed, unchangeable conceptions which embrace them all. Here, simultaneously, is simplification and stabilization.

The new pattern of the Dominate as it was revealed in life itself, appears, as we have seen, *explicite*—in what can be seen with our own eyes and therefore with greatest perspicuity—in the contemporary art and architecture. Above (pp. 9 ff.), in a general survey of the transformation of building forms toward Late Antiquity, we have seen how a new conception of structure is developed in architecture. More specifically we will concentrate our comments upon the new solutions to problems of form which came about in the time around A.D. 300, after the tetrarchic state had overcome the great crisis of the second half of the third century. We shall encounter compositions which can be described with words very like those used to characterize the constitutional organization of the tetrarchic state and its administrative system. We will first examine the imperial palace and from there pass on to the Christian basilica. Thereafter we will look at figurative art. Here, above all, two groups of monuments have left to us a body of material from the period around 300 sufficient for a study in detail of the transformation of form which took place during this critical period: the first of these groups is sculptured reliefs upon sarcophagi and public monuments; the second, portrait sculpture.

THE IMPERIAL PALACE AND THE BASILICA

In the development of the Roman imperial palace we see—in accordance with the whole basic tendency in the architectural development during the Roman Empire (pp. 13 ff.)—how a rather free disposition of the building units gives way to strictly bound axial compositions, the individual parts of which are, in a more or less heavy-handed manner, symmetrically arranged. The more open, villa-like palace architecture of earlier times becomes enclosed in fortresslike blocks.

The best preserved of all the Roman imperial palaces, Diocletian's palace in Spalato on the Dalmatian coast (Fig. 23), illustrates the new palace type of the Dominate.[1] While in earlier tradition—exemplified by the imperial palaces on the Palatine and in Hadrian's palace at Tivoli—the ground plan and the elevation may show great irregularity in that new parts grow organically out of the older, Diocletian's palace is a closed stereometric block of mathematic regularity, with a ground plan of

[1] G. Niemann, *Der Palast Diokletians in Spalato*, Vienna, 1910.

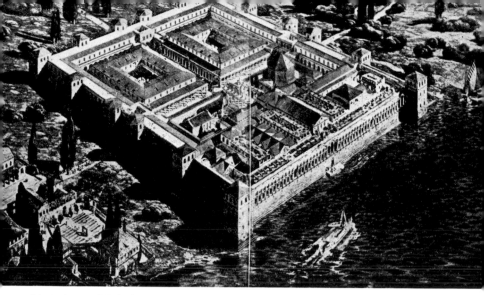

23. Palace of Diocletian in Spalato, reconstruction (Niemann)

rectangles arranged according to a strict coordinate system. It is fixed in each part, unchangeably stipulated on a geometric formula, thus without possibility of further growth and development. Here is the same contrast between free grouping and mechanical coordination, between organic growth from within and symmetrical stabilization imposed from above, as that which we have indicated as characteristic in all relations between the Principate and the Dominate. Let us examine Diocletian's palace at Spalato more closely.

The ground plan of the palace is approximately rectangular and in each of the four corners of the rectangle is placed a mighty tower. The side of the rectangle which faces the sea, is formed as the façade; the three other sides, facing land, are formed as fortified walls secured by towers closing off the palace from the land. Lengthwise, through the whole palace runs a main axis from a tower-flanked portal at the center of the landward side to a three-bay columned opening at the center of the side facing the sea. At a right angle to this main axis, a transversal axis cuts through the palace, running from a tower-flanked portal at the center of one length of the palace rectangle to a tower-flanked portal at the center of the other. Along these two axes, which form a cross, are built columned streets. The longitudinal axis is clearly marked out as the main axis: in this axis, provision is made in constantly rising architectural movements for the most holy suite of rooms for the imperial ceremonials (*palatium sacrum*) with columned atrium, vestibule, and throne room. The four rectangles formed by the main axes are again subdivided into rectangular units, all firmly enclosed within the coordinate system of the palace rectangle: the whole, a composition at right angles, along horizontal and vertical lines and dominated by the quadratic-rectangular framework—everything corresponding to the new pattern of composition we shall find in the pictorial art of that time (p. 90).

That the palace at Spalato is clearly symptomatic of the time is shown by Diocletian's palace in Palmyra on the Eufrates.[2] As in Spalato, the palace in Palmyra is cut by crossed axes of wide, columned streets which, as at Spalato, run between fortified gates. In Palmyra also the columned street forming the longitudinal axis marks the main axis and leads into the great columned atrium in front of the ceremonial suite of the palace. As at Spalato, the large rectangular building units into which the palace is divided are enclosed within the coordinate system of the crossed axes. The ceremonial suite again lies at the rear of the whole plan, but in Palmyra it rises majestically upon a high, built-up terrace above the steeply falling terrain upon which the other buildings are symmetrically regulated according to the main axis.

[2] Th. Wiegand, *Palmyra*, Berlin, 1932, pl. 10; cf. D. Krencker, *ibid.*, pp. 84 ff., and H. Lehner, *ibid.*, p. 160: interpretation of the complex as a palace. Newest excavation of the building by K. Michalowski and discussion by D. Schlumberger, *Mélanges Monterdi*, II (1962), pp. 79 ff. and by E. Will, in *Syria*, 40, 1963, pp. 385 ff.

Transformations in the Art and Architecture

This palace architecture of Diocletian is clearly influenced by Roman military architecture. The rectangular plan of the palace at Spalato, its fortified walls and crossed axial streets connecting the gates at the center of each side: all this belongs inseparably to the Roman fortified camp, the *castrum*. Such a fusion of *castrum* into the architecture of the imperial palace is in strict accord with the militarization of state and administration—indeed, of the whole style of life—which took place during the third century (pp. 7 f.). Where before, Greek names—Academy, Lyceum, etc.—were used to indicate the different parts of the palace, now the word *praetorium*—i.e., the headquarters of the camp commander—became the common term designating the main building in the palace precinct. It is a development toward the fortified palace of the Middle Ages, the fortress, where the palace lives on in the castle—as the word itself, *palatium*, survives in the mediaeval term *Pfalz*. Swoboda refers to a number of eastern examples of this militarization of the palace buildings during Late Antiquity and the early Middle Ages, for example, to the Byzantine Kasr Ibn Wardan in northern Syria, from the sixth century A.D., and to Arabian desert castles such as Mschatta. In Kasr Ibn Wardan the palace had become "a cubic crystal of a building enlivened only by the windows which break the wall surfaces."[3]

The nucleus of the imperial palace was a suite of rooms dedicated to the imperial ceremonials. With the increasing importance of the emperor cult in Late Antiquity, this ceremonial suite attains a more and more dominating position in the imperial palace: it becomes the holy of holies, the *palatium sacrum*, where the emperor himself

[3] K. M. Swoboda, *Römische und Romanische Paläste*, Vienna, 1919, fig. 70, p. 56. Cf. Alföldi, "Insignen," *Mitteilungen des Deutschen Archaeolog. Instituts, Röm. Abt.*, 50, 1935, p. 46.

is enthroned in his throne room like a divine image of worship.[4] In Diocletian's palace in Spalato, this *palatium sacrum* received the form which was to become the prototype for the palaces of the Dominate.[5] Let us examine it more closely.

From the land façade, as we have seen, a broad, columned street runs along the main axis of the palace and after crossing the transversal columned street, it leads into the ceremonial suite. This consists of the large columned court (*atrium*), which continues the axis of the columned street and ends with a three-bay, columned gable-pediment at the back; beneath this gable, which is a gable of glorification, the emperor appears before those gathered in the atrium (Fig. 24). Behind the gable is a circular, domed vestibule and behind this lies the throne room itself, the *triclinium*, all in the same axis. The rear of the throne room opens onto a portico at the center of the sea façade of the palace; here the emperor appeared, again in the same commanding ceremonial axis, at the middle of the sea façade where he stood with a great three-bay, columned opening framing his divine person as did the glorification gable in the atrium when he emerged from the throne room in the opposite direction.

The large, columned atrium was the gathering place for the court—even today the name court is derived from this open courtyard in the imperial palaces of Late Antiquity: court, *cour, corte, Hof*—and when, from the inner halls of the ceremonial suite, the emperor appeared under the glorification gable, those assembled in the columned court sank to their knees before the God-Emperor. The privileged, who were granted audience in the

---

[4] Alföldi, *op.cit.*, pp. 127 ff.

[5] Fundamental for the study of late antique imperial palace architecture are the works by E. Dyggve, cf. his *Ravennatum Palatium Sacrum*, Copenhagen, 1941, and, *Dödekult, keiserkult og basilika*, Copenhagen, 1943.

throne room, assembled first in the domed vestibule behind the glorification gable. From there they proceeded, surrounded by the chamberlains and officials of the imperial ritual, into the throne room and waited there, in a mysterious *silentium*, the moment when the heavy draperies which hung down before the holy of holies in the rear of the throne room would be drawn aside—these curtains which in the language of the Byzantine court poetry are called "clouds which conceal the light of heaven." The clouds part and the sun shines forth: those seeking audience see the God-Emperor enthroned before them beneath his columned baldachin, the ciborium (compare Fig. 25), surrounded by lighted torches, shining in gold and silver, glittering with jewels and with the godly light radiating around his head, *lux divinum verticem clare orbe complectens.*[6] All fall to their knees and hymns, shouts of praise, and acclamations resound throughout the hall.

Around this *palatium sacrum* in the main axis of the palace, the architectural elements are symmetrically arranged, not unlike, as we shall see, the way in which all the figurative elements in the contemporary imperial art are symmetrically disposed around the emperor to whom they all are subordinated (Figs. 35 f., 48 f.). For one walking down the columned street towards the atrium, the emperor-axis was marked by the imposing columned gable at the rear of the atrium and by the cupola which towers behind the gable. The mausoleum of the Jupiter-Emperor and the Temple of Jupiter which lie directly opposite one another on each side of the atrium, are both subject to the order of this palace axis—even the Temple of Jupiter! Octavian, the first augustus, had already constructed in connection with his own *domus* a temple to his patron god, namely, the Temple of Apollo on the

[6] *Mamertini paneg. Max.*, 3. Cf. the portrait of Theodosius, Fig. 24.

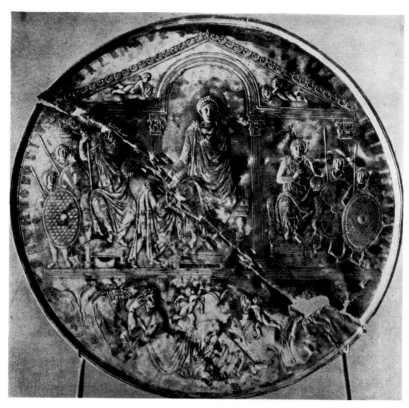

24. Emperor-image of Theodosius, Madrid (Delbrück)

Palatine; however, he had subordinated his *domus* to the temple. In Diocletian's palace the relationship has changed; it is now the imperial suite which is superior, everything is regulated according to the emperor-axis, the symmetric order of the Dominate.

In these axially dominated imperial suites even the figurative decoration is now regulated according to the emperor-axis. A splendid example of how the figurative decoration accompanies the ascending order throughout the succession of rooms in the ceremonial suite is found in the floor mosaics of the recently excavated palace in Piazza Armerina in Sicily (Fig. 26), which has been much discussed by archaeologists and historians as to date and interpretation during recent years. In our opinion the

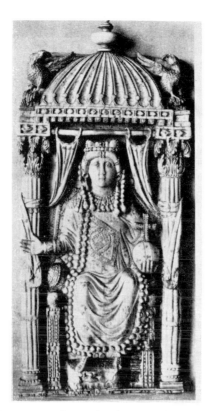

25. Empress beneath ciborium (Delbrück)

ceremonial suites are to be dated around A.D. 300 and
may have been built by Diocletian's co-augustus, Maxi-
mianus Herculeus.[7] The porticos of the atria in both the

[7] This interpretation has been approved by G. V. Gentili, the excava-
tor of the palace. Presumably it was a retirement palace for the abdicated
Maximian, thus a parallel to the retirement palace in Spalato for Maximian's imperial colleague, Diocletian: L'Orange-Dyggve, "'E' un palazzo di Massimiano Erculio che gli scavi di Piazza Armerina portano alla
luce?", *Symbolae Osloenses*, 29, 1952, pp. 114 ff. L'Orange, "Il palazzo
di Massimiano Erculio di Piazza Armerina," *Studi in onore di Aristide
Calderini e Roberto Paribeni*, III, 1956; *Idem*, "Nuovo contributo allo
studio del Palazzo di Piazza Armerina," *Acta Instituti Romani Nor-
vegiae*, Rome, 2, 1965 (in press). G. V. Gentili, *La Villa Erculia di
Piazza Armerina, I mosaici figurati*, Rome, 1959. Also approved by I.
Lavin, "The Hunting Mosaics of Antioch," *Dumbarton Oaks Papers*,
1963, pp. 244 ff. Objections to this interpretation of the palace have

ceremonial suites are covered with a mosaic carpet with images of wild animals—heads, protomes, beasts in rinceau —most of them belonging to the arena. In the larger of the two suites, the vestibule that forms a sort of narrow narthex between the atrium and the throne room gives us the next movement in the mosaic decoration: the wild beasts, shown here entire and in their natural surroundings, are hunted by the imperial huntsmen, captured, and transported over the sea to the arena. The enormous mosaic which measures more than 60 meters in length, shows in the dominating central scene, which is placed in the very axis of the ceremonial suite, *four men* with the typical tetrarchical vestments and insignia: thus the tetrarchical state and administration is manifest in the picture. The hunting scenes seek to comprise all the wild beasts of the east and the west, the north and the south, as the imperial games had to embrace *omnia in toto orbe animalia,* to demonstrate the universality of the Empire.

The blood bath of the amphitheater emanates from these pictures even while they convey the genuine antique idea of the heroic slaughter of animals, the triumph over "the beast," the idea of the great subduer of wild monsters, Hercules. In the closing movement of the pictorial decoration, in the very throne room itself, this Hercules idea is extolled in clear figures and symbols to the one entering. Here, in the smaller of the two ceremonial suites, we see the "labors" of Hercules presented as an accomplished fact—the slaughtered or captured animals

been made by B. Pace, *I mosaici di Piazza Armerina,* Rome, 1955; by M. Cagiano de Azevedo, "I proprietari della villa di Piazza Armerina," *Scritti di storia dell'arte in onore di Mario Salmi,* 1961, pp. 18 ff.; by G. Lugli, "Contributo alla storia edilizia della villa romana di Piazza Armerina," *Rivista dell'Istituto Naz. d'Archeologia e storia dell'arte,* Nuova Serie XI-XII, Rome, 1963, pp. 28 ff. The palace itself has collapsed, but the ground plan and the floor mosaics have been preserved. Originally also the walls and the vaults were adorned with mosaics.

and monsters, the Hydra, the Cerberus, the Nemean lion, etc., lie scattered about us. The symbolism is carried even further: we see Hercules crowned by Jupiter. The whole pictorial decoration reaches its final culmination in the central apse. Here, at the "high point" of the emperor-axis is portrayed the *gigantomachia*, the Olympians' fight against the world rebellion of the giants, a battle which Jupiter could only win with the help of Hercules. At the corresponding place in the larger ceremonial suite stood a colossal statue of Hercules.[8]

In reality it is the Emperor himself who is revealed in this progressive interpretation of the Hercules idea. The emperor himself is the heroic hunter; Hercules-emperors, as for example Commodus, could therefore take direct part in the animal slaughter of the arena. In such hunts was revealed the victorious power which invincibly strikes down all the evil "beasts" that threaten human order: the power which is constantly active in the *praesens Hercules*, Maximian (p. 52). The greatest manifestation of this power is shown in the victory over the mutinous powers of earth, the children of Gaia, who arise from the elements against the heavenly Olympus. In this mythical picture the warring emperors receive—both in figurative art and in the panegyrics[9]—their highest realization, in that the *gigantomachia*, in which Jupiter and Hercules fling the destructive powers of the earth into the depths of Tartaros, is the uniting symbol of the two imperial dynasties.

The same strict axial disposition of the room units into the same ascending order of rank toward the holy of

[8] L'Orange, "Il palazzo di Massimiano Erculio . . . ," *Studi in onore di Calderini e Paribeni*, p. 596, with illustrations.

[9] The emperors as Jupiter and Hercules in the gigantomachia: for example, *Mamertini paneg. Max.*, 4; *Mamertini gencthl. Max.*, 3.

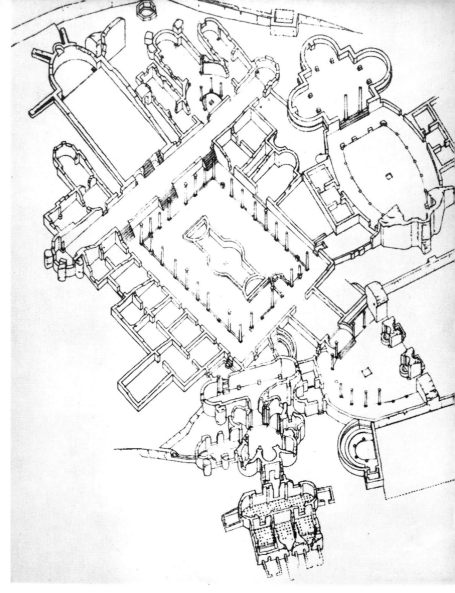

26. Palace at Piazza Armerina (Gismondi)

holies, and the same firm symmetrical grouping of the separate building parts around this axis, is repeated in the "normal-basilical" church architecture created under Constantine the Great, which in Rome is represented by

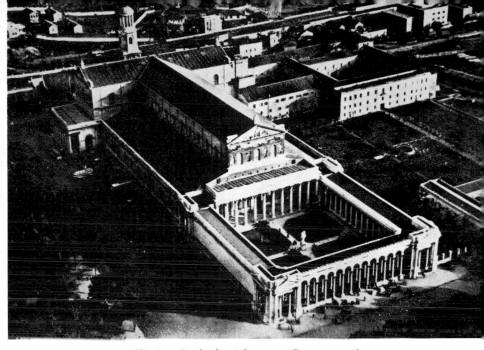

27. San Paolo fuori le mura, Rome, exterior

such monumental complexes as the Christ Church (now
St. John's Church) in the Lateran, Old St. Peter's, San
Paolo fuori le Mura, and Santa Maria Maggiore (Figs.
27-30) and which afterwards lives on in simplified forms
in the mediaeval basilica of Rome. While previously the
Christian basilica was thought to be derived from the
antique market-basilica, modern scholars emphasize the
differences between the market and the Christian normal-
basilica. The market-basilica, which is dedicated to secu-
lar and everyday life, stretches along the side of the
market as a sort of architectural addition to it, a kind of
market under a roof. In the Christian basilica, on the
other hand, which is dedicated to the Christian cult, the
entire architecture is axially directed toward the center of
the cult in the rear, toward the altar, glorified under its
celestial baldachin, the ciborium: precisely in the same
way in which the imperial *palatium sacrum* was oriented
axially toward its cult center, the enthroned emperor

81

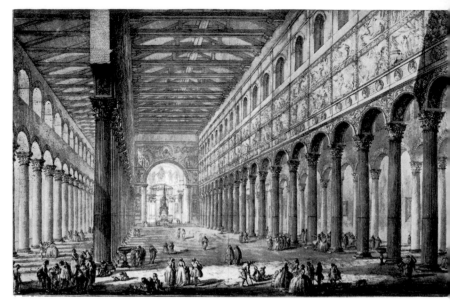

28. San Paolo fuori le mura, Rome, interior

under the ciborium. Indeed it is just these fixed architectural elements of the imperial *palatium sacrum*—first the open atrium at the front of the palace, then the vast covered assembly hall before the holy of holies, and further, a number of glorifying architectural forms such as the glorification gable and the ciborium—which recur in more or less remodeled form in the Christian normal-basilica of Constantine.[10] The sacral architectural forms which framed and glorified the appearance of the God-Emperor before the people, are taken over and sublimated in the Christian normal-basilica, which framed and glorified the presence of the celestial King in the sacraments—the altar of the Lord.

Along the longitudinal axis we walk first through the open, columned atrium, then through a vestibule (*narthex*), then through the covered basilica—all corresponding to the arrangement in the *palatium sacrum*. The wide

[10] E. Dyggve, *Dödekult, keiserkult og basilika*, Copenhagen, 1943; *Palatium sacrum Ravennatum*, Copenhagen, 1941, *passim*.

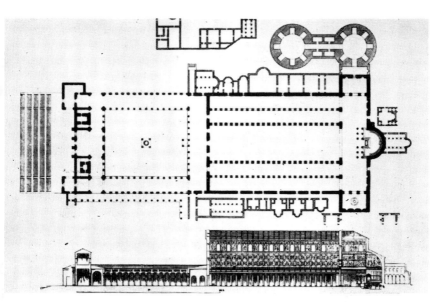

29. Old St. Peter's, Rome

and lofty nave between narrower and lower aisles in the
covered basilica, runs between rows of columns, like a
via triumphalis, towards the apse at the other side of the
transept. In front of the transept this columned street
passes under a triumphal arch that rests upon the axis of
the complex no differently than the glorification gable
rests upon the axis of the imperial palace. From the nave
one looks through this columned portal, which focuses
all eyes upon the "apex" of the axial line, the altar, and
the ciborium in the apse. Three heavens—the triumphal
arch, the apse vault, the ciborium vault—extend in glory
above this altar. Both nave and transept have an open
timber roof, only the triumphal arch, the apse niche and
the ciborium are vaulted; therefore the eye is drawn to
the altar which they frame; everything is arranged according to the altar-axis which here replaces the emperor-
axis of the *palatium sacrum.*

All the architectural elements tend toward symmetrical
grouping around this axis. The columns may differ as
the movement glides forward through each separate row

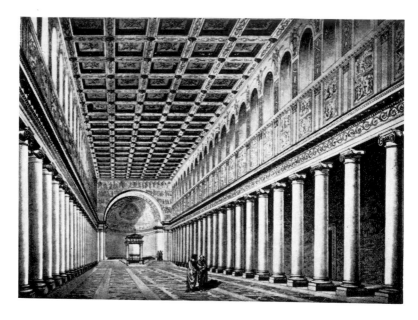

30. Santa Maria Maggiore, Rome

of columns, but the columns opposite one another are usually alike, thus forming symmetrical pairs on either side of the axis. In each pair the columns thus usually have the same type of capital, and they increase in magnificence as they approach the holy of holies.[11] This conscious directing of all the elements from the cult center forms a precise analogy to the symmetrical arrangements in contemporary figurative art. If, in imitation of what occurs there (pp. 94 f.), one turned each of the two rows of columns framing the nave 90 degrees to each side into the plane of the triumphal arch so that they formed wings on each side of it, the columns, with their changing capitals, would form ever-changing symmetric pairs around the cult center which emerges under the triumphal arch, similar to the way in which the figures in representational

[11] F. W. Deichmann, "Säule und Ordnung in der frühchristl. Architektur," *Mitteilungen des Deutschen Archäolog. Instituts, Röm. Abt.* 55, 1940, pp. 121 ff.; idem, *Frühchristliche Kirchen in Rom*, Basel, 1948, pp. 12 ff.

Transformations in the Art and Architecture

images form varying symmetrical pairs around the central figure.

The whole decoration of the church interior, the encrustation and the ornamentation of the walls, the covering of the individual parts with gold, silver, colored glass, etc., follows the ascending line towards the apse, and in the same measure on both sides of the axis. Again, as we found in the imperial *palatium sacrum*, this applies also to the figurative decoration. The great culmination is found at the "apex" of the axis where Christ himself, like Hercules in Piazza Armerina, appears in all his might. Towards this representation of Christ the whole pictorial decoration of the basilica is directed with increasing momentum and according to the laws of axiality.

THE PICTORIAL RELIEF

As an example of the classical pictorial composition that lived on for a long time in the art of the Principate, we choose a well-known relief medallion from the period of Emperor Hadrian (a.d. 118-136), which was used two hundred years after it was made to decorate the Roman Triumphal Arch of Constantine (Fig. 31). Hadrian has just finished his hunt and, followed by his hunting companions, steps up to the statue of Apollo and pours his offering upon the flaming altar at the foot of the statue. Here, the classical tradition of form is alive not only in the magnificent plastic modeling of the bodies but also in the ideal proportioning of the figures and in the way the weight of the body has been placed on one foot while the other is unburdened, the whole figure thereby receiving its swinging curve in a freedom which, as far back as the fifth century b.c., gives to the portrayal of man in classical art its typical expression of calm, relaxed naturalness. Equally characteristic of the classical tradition of form is the arrangement of the figures: they are

85

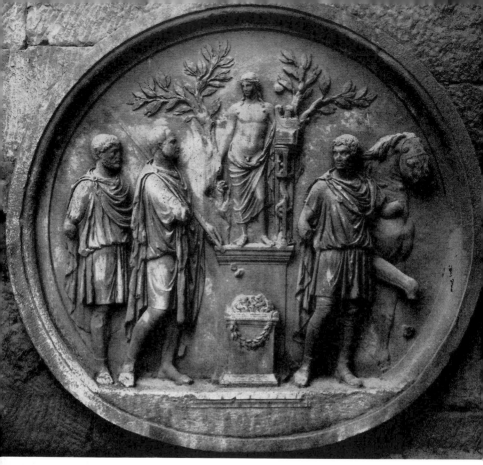

31. Hadrianic medallion, Arch of Constantine, Rome

32. Circus sarcophagus, Foligno, Umbria. Second part of
   III cent. A.D.

33. Prometheus sarcophagus, National Museum, Naples.
   Second part of III cent. A.D.

34. Sarcophagus with myth of Phaethon, Giardino del Lago,
   Villa Borghese, Rome. Second part of III cent. A.D.

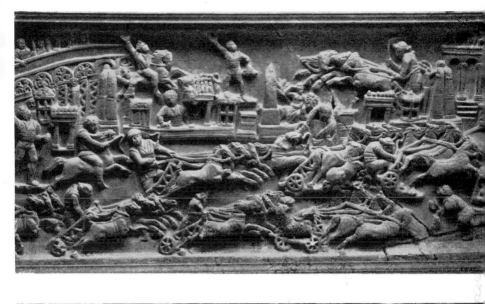

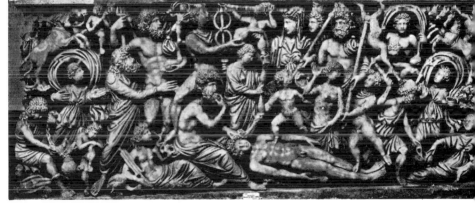

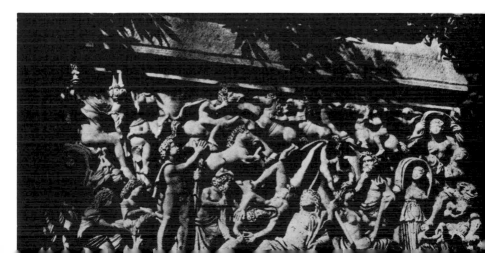

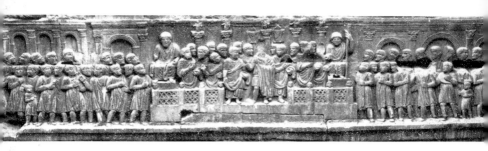

35. *Oratio*. Relief on the Arch of Constantine, Rome, A.D. 312-315

separated from each other in order that each body may be seen in itself as an organic unit and a corporeally beautiful whole; at the same time they are, by their position, movement, and gesture, placed in a certain rhythmic mutual relationship, a certain reciprocal contact which causes us to perceive them as an organic, living group.

In the development which takes place during the critical third century, this classical composition is shattered. At the same time as the disintegration of the Empire and the general social and economic disorganization (pp. 39 ff.), there takes place in art a characteristic destruction of traditional form. One may choose examples of this among the circus, the Prometheus and Phaethon sarcophagi of that period (Figs. 32-34). The figures lose their corporeal beauty and no longer exist in organic groupings. They overlap and cover one another in such a way that they no longer appear as organic units but rather as parts of entwined tangles of figures. The organic groups of harmonically related figures are replaced by turbulent throngs of entwined but contrasting figures. The contours of the figures no longer flow rhythmically, but are formed by straight and jagged lines, somewhat spasmodically; characteristic are the abrupt, marionette-like movements. With distinctive exaggeration of gestures, movements, and mimicry, the confrontation of the individual figures is rich in contrast and drama. We are faced with singularly excited and harried, peculiarly dis-

88

integrated compositions with a strangely glimmering and flickering life.[12] One may speak of anarchy of form.

Toward the end of the third century and during the first decades of the fourth, the disconnected pictorial elements are collected into a new compositional order. But, as in the contemporary tetrarchic reorganization of state and civic life, the new order in art is not, as in the classical tradition, an organic order based upon free figures in spontaneous groupings, but a *mechanical* order imposed upon objects from above, regulating their mutual relationship—an order which is based upon a higher regularity than that of nature. If we look at the two well-known reliefs on the façade of the Arch of Constantine (312 315)—namely *Oratio*, i.e., Constantine's speech on the Rostra at the Forum Romanum (Fig. 35), and *Liberalitas*, i.e., Constantine's distribution of a gift of money to the citizens of Rome (Fig. 36)—we will find this new mechanical order fully developed: the separate figures are not gathered in free, natural groups, but are

[12] The art of the Tetrarchy and the late third century was, on the basis of then unpublished material, analyzed and characterized in my work *Studien zur Geschichte des spätantiken Porträts*, Instituttet for sammenlignende Kulturforskning, Oslo, 1933. The sarcophagi of that period have, above all, been treated in German research, G. Rodenwaldt, F. Gerke, Fr. Matz, H. von Schoenebeck, cf. bibliography in L'Orange—von Gerkan, *Der spätantike Bildschmuck des Konstantinbogens*, Berlin, 1939, p. 207, note 4; cf. also Rodenwaldt, *op.cit.*, CAH, XII, 1939, p. 558. In the work already mentioned on the Arch of Constantine, pp. 192 ff., I have presented the material on which my analysis of the stylistic development in that work and in the present study is based.

36. *Liberalitas*. Relief on the Arch of Constantine, Rome, A.D. 312-315

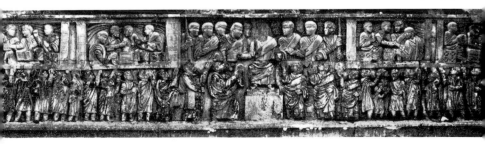

arranged as uniform elements side by side in rows; neither these rows nor the architecture that frames them are free, but everything is strictly subordinated to and symmetrized according to the dominating figure of the Emperor at the center of the relicf; the compelling regularity which row and symmetry impose upon the figures, is increased by the fact that the axes of the whole composition conform to the horizontals and verticals of the framework. The main lines in the figures and architecture represented either coincide with or are parallel to the framework—for example, the line just above the head of the figures and that just under the feet. The new compositional system is thus characterized by row formations, symmetry, and the total subordination to the ordinates of the framework: an organization of form that completely corresponds to the structure of the Dominate. At the same time that the individual figure loses its well-proportioned, organic integrity, and becomes straightened out according to the verticals of the framework the tradi-

37. Detail of *Oratio* in Fig. 35

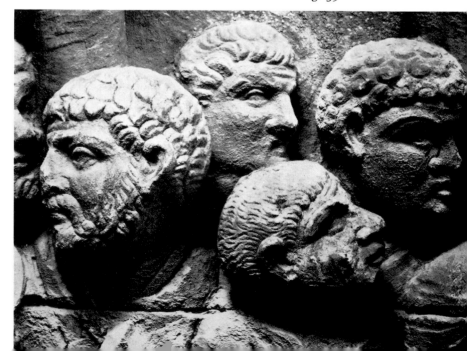

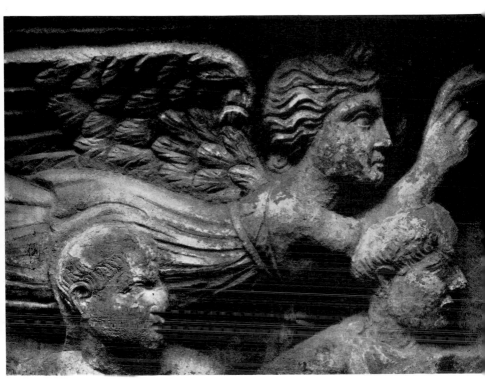

38. Detail of a relief on the Arch of Constantine, A.D. 312-315

tional curve of the figure at ease disappears and thereby the genuine classical expression of idle, relaxed humanity.

There is a mechanical anchoring of the form down to even the smallest detail. Where a surface presents the possibility for a freer use of form—for example, in the rendering of hair and feathers, of water and stone—it is usual to repeat regularly the same form-motif. In distinct contrast to the tumultuous effervescence of hair and beard, horse's mane etc., from the end of the third century, there appears the monotonous dividing and stratifying of the locks in the reliefs on the Arch of Constantine (Fig. 37) or on contemporary Early Christian sarcophagi. We find everywhere the same mechanical partitioning of the form, for example, in the rendering of the feathers on Victory's wings and of the folds of her

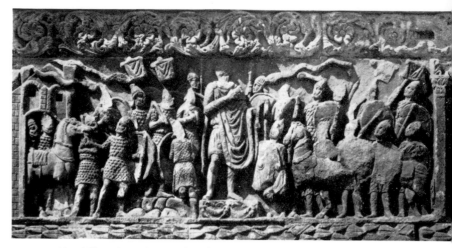

39. *Adlocutio militum* of Galerius. Relief on the Arch of Galerius, Thessalonika, ca. A.D. 300

drapery (Fig. 38). Most striking in this abstract regularity is the way in which rock formations are rendered in the form of a honeycomb (Fig. 47: lower angle).

Particularly characteristic of the new type of composition is the mechanical unity achieved by symmetry which around the year 300 replaces the organic unity achieved by living group formations. In the reliefs on the Arch of Galerius in Thessalonika, from ca. A.D. 300, the endeavor is manifest to symmetrize the composition around the Emperor, or the Emperors. In the representation of the *Adlocutio Militum* of Galerius (Fig. 39), the whole pyramidal composition is topped by the head of the Emperor; his mighty body, arising powerfully above the surrounding figures, is placed in the middle of the two wings of soldiers, in rows gradually sloping downwards. In the composition one perceives the strong lines of an isosceles triangle with its apex, the Emperor's head.

In the four-emperor relief on the same arch (Fig. 40) the symmetry penetrates even deeper into the whole construction of the composition. The group of Emperors takes the dominating central position in the picture; at the center are the two augusti enthroned, each upon his heavenly vault formed by a drapery arched dome-like over a bust of a sky-god; each has his assisting caesar beside him and they are both being crowned by a small Victory hovering between the caesars and augusti. In the side-fields the figures are made symmetric around the central group, as is evident in the reclining figure in each corner—Oceanus in the left, Tellus in the right—and in the figures hastening towards the emperors—Rome on the left, Mars on the right. In spite of their difference as iconographic types, these last two gods correspond to each other symmetrically in their position, movement, attributes (trophy and helmet), as do also the figures that frame them.

We find similar symmetrical compositions on contemporary sarcophagi; for example, a sarcophagus from ca. A.D. 300, in the Terme Museum, Rome (Fig. 41). The turbulent, excited life of the departing third century is still present in the fluttering individual forms, in the sharp, jerky movements, and in the wind-blown hair and drapery forms. All the more remarkable is the unmistakable effort to bring the whole composition to rest in a symmetric order. At the center of the relief stands the main figure: the toga-clad deceased. All the other components of the relief—the two banner-bearers (*vexillarii*), the trophies—are placed symmetrically around the central figure as corresponding, objectively homo-

40. Four-Emperor relief on the Arch of Galerius, Thessalonika, ca. A.D. 300

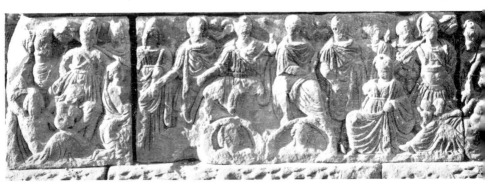

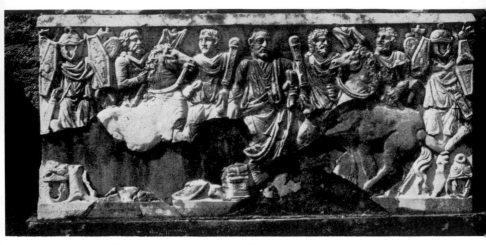

41. Sarcophagus, Terme Museum, Rome, ca. A.D. 300

geneous pairs. The iron grip of symmetry and the uniformness of the figures within the separate symmetrical pairs
are carried through also in the details, as can be seen,
for example, in the swords of the soldiers, the *vexilla*, and
in the swords hanging on the two trophies.

A good ten years later, as seen in the reliefs on the
Arch of Constantine discussed above, the symmetric
crystallization of the composition is complete. In both
Oratio and *Liberalitas* the Emperor appears—elevated
upon the Rostra or sitting upon his high throne—as the
dominating central figure, with rows of acclaiming and
jubilant figures surrounding him symmetrically and subordinated to him. In *Liberalitas* (Fig. 36) the central
section with the Emperor enthroned above the cubic
pedestal, is framed by perfectly symmetric architectural
settings on either side. The structures are divided into
a first and a second story, and the second story is again
divided into two completely equal loggia-like rooms,
where the symmetry is extended also to the furnishings.
Indeed, even the human figures represented in the two
loggias of the two side sections—four male figures who
take part in the distributing and receiving of the imperial

gift—are subject to the same law of symmetry (Figs. 42, 43). On the floor in the middle, between the four active figures, stands a coffer full of money. In the part of the loggia which lies farthest to the right in the right-hand section, and in the corresponding part to the left in the left-hand section, a man wearing a paenula comes out of a hatchway from the story below and protrudes halfway into the loggia to receive the gift of money in his paenula. Opposite him in the other corner of the loggia, a high state official in the toga is sitting on a chair, holding a diptycon or a scroll. Before him a lower official, wearing a simple tunic, empties the gift of money from a tray into the paenula of the recipient. Between this official and the recipient appears still another high official, again in the toga. The whole complicated scene with roll call and accounting, distribution and receipt of the monetary gift, is repeated thus in each loggia according to exactly the same pattern, and on both sides of the enthroned emperor at the center of the relief the self-same pattern is reversed, in keeping with the laws of symmetry.[13]

The acclaiming citizens who fill the lower zone in both wings of the picture both in *Oratio* and in *Liberalitas*, as noted above, do not stand in natural groupings in free and open space, but are placed side by side against the firm plane of the ground—in *Oratio* in two parallel rows (Fig. 44), in *Liberalitas* in one single row (Fig. 36). Because the figures are thus placed side by side, not gliding behind one another in depth and disappearing into the background, they all appear with the same substantial weight and fullness, with the same degree of volume. Thus one could say that they appear as equal units. This impression is further strengthened by the avoidance, as far as possible, of rhythmic contractions or dispersions of the figures. No melodic undulating movement goes

[13] L'Orange—von Gerkan, *op.cit.*, pp. 89 ff. Pls. 5 b, 16, 17, 22.

95

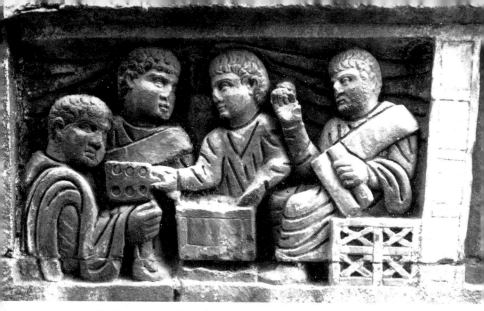

42. Detail of *Liberalitas* in Fig. 36: loggia farthest left

through these rows of figures, only the monotonous
cadence of equal units.[14] The uniformity of the figures
is accentuated also by the arrangement of the individuals
in the row according to the same horizontal axes: their
heads, feet, etc., are on the same line. Particularly in the
two parallel rows in *Oratio* (Fig. 44) do the figures
unite, between distinct horizontal lines, to form a compact mass, and they rise like parallel walls one above another. Such solid masses of figures were to the organic
figure-groups of classical times as the collective corporations of the Dominate are to the free organizations of the
earlier Empire.

The emphasizing of horizontal dividing dominants
of this kind derives from a totally new order of form
which—as we saw it above—subordinates the whole
pictorial scenery to the coordinate system of the frame.
The horizontal and vertical lines of the frame exercise a

[14] Cf. G. Rodenwaldt, "Reihung identischer Glieder," *SBBerl*, 1933,
pp. 1036 f.

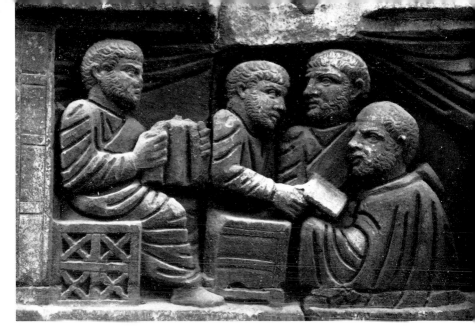

13. Detail of *Liberalitas* in Fig. 36: loggia farthest right

new compulsion upon the composition of both the architectural and figurative scenes. Thus, for example, in *Liberalitas*, the framing fillets of the relief determine the divisions into the loggia-formed enclosures. And with similar effect the architectural elements in the *Oratio* are made parallel with the rectangle of the frame—indeed, the accentuated horizontal line of the upper edge of the background architecture coincides partly with the fillet of the relief's frame. But also the whole scene of figures is made to conform with the vertical and horizontal lines of the frame. It is, for example, remarkable how in the double row of figures in both wings of *Oratio*, each row is enclosed in a rectangle conforming to the framework; particularly marked is the horizontal line formed by the crowns of the heads in each rectangle. It is no coincidence that the block joint running through the middle of the whole relief and forming a dominating horizontal dividing line coincides with and sets off the line formed by the

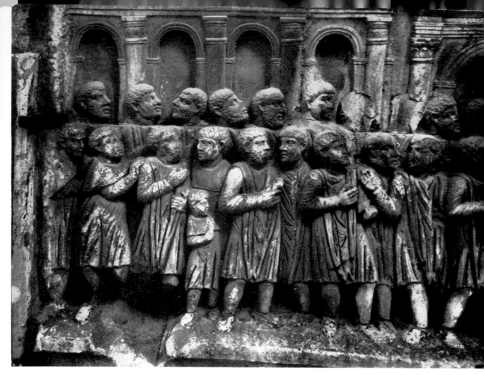

44. Left wing of *Oratio* in Fig. 35

crowns of the heads in the lower row (Fig. 44). If one studies the single figures on the reliefs of the Arch of Constantine, as for example the hovering Victories with trophies in the spandrels of the main archway (Figs. 45-46), one may realize the power that the outer frame exercises in the whole design. The upper part of the body is straightened as vertically as possible, while the lower part of the body swings out horizontally, and the trophy in Victory's hands bends concentrically with the curved frame of the arch underneath. Also in a peculiar stair-like construction (for example, Fig. 47) the figures are made to conform to the frame. *The weaker the organic integrity of the figure, the greater the pliancy of its separate parts toward the force of the outer framework*: we have found analogous the relationship in contemporary life between individuals and community, between the city and the provinces on the one side and the fixed blocks of the new state on the other. As a post-Constantinian example of this total subordination of all the figure elements under the coordinates of the framework, we reproduce here two reliefs on the base of the Theodosius Obelisk on the hippodrome in Constantinople (Figs. 48, 49).

We emphasize finally how characteristic the absence of open space around the figures is for the entire expression in these compositions. The figure is bound to the row, just as the soldier to his rank or file, and the row in turn to the narrow space before the plane of the ground. The figures are restricted to this narrow space; they can neither press forward toward the viewer nor recede into the depths of a background.[15] The only poo

[15] In *Oratio* the breaking down of the natural space and the mechanical division of it into layers parallel to the background is particularly noticeable. As the locality here represented, namely the Forum Romanum, is still preserved, the artist's transformation of it can be analyzed in a very concrete way. We see in the background the buildings which frame the Forum, from right to left the Arch of Septimius-Severus, the Rostra, the Arch of Tiberius, the Basilica Julia. While in reality the Basilica Julia is placed at a right angle to the Rostra and the fronts of the two arches, in the relief it is projected into the plane of the relief and receives the same front as the other three monuments. Thus the four buildings do not enclose, as in reality, a three-dimensional space, but are arranged into one *stratum* parallel with the ground of the relief. As with the Forum architecture, so also with the crowds which fill the space enclosed by the buildings. Of course, these crowds, who are listening to Constantine's speech from the Rostra, in reality are gathered together in the large open space in front of the Rostra and push forth in depth toward the speaker. However, to avoid the natural development in depth, the artist projects the crowd into the plane and places the figures at each side of the Rostra where it divides into double rows in narrow strata parallel to the ground. In effect it is precisely the same which has occurred in *Liberalitas*. The architecture of the two wings should, in reality, be seen in perspective, parallel to each other, leading in towards the emperor and senators in an apse-like termination at the end of the room. And again, the crowds of people who throng

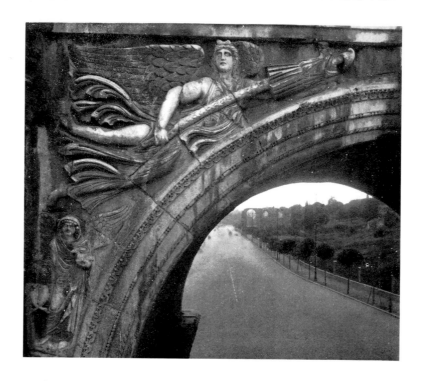

sible movement is along the axis of a plane parallel to
the ground; but in this plane any movement is prevented
by the symmetric order which keeps the figures firmly in
position, subordinated to the central figure. Thus, in a
peculiar way the figures are *immobilized*—just as in real
life individuals were firmly tied by the Dominate to their
state duties, their *munera*, the place of their employment
and property (pp. 4 f.).

Row formations of the type we are studying, accom-
modate and simplify the symmetrical arrangement of
the composition and strengthen the expression of subordination to the central figure. In quite a different way
than in traditional art where the figures moved more

together in the large open space before the emperor and between the
loggia-constructions, are projected into the plane and placed to both
sides of the enthroned Majesty dividing into rows parallel with the
plane of the ground. Cf. L'Orange—von Gerkan, *op.cit.*, pp. 81, 86
f., 98.

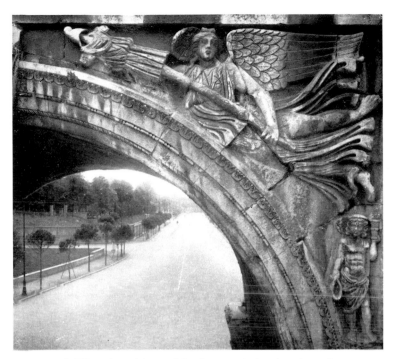

45.46. Victories with trophies in spandrels of main archway,
Arch of Constantine, A.D. 312 315

freely in space, it now becomes possible to direct all the
elements towards the emperor in the center, in order to
experience the irresistible magnetic charge emanating
from him and the higher order to which he belongs. It
is the divine Empire which is represented in this supernatural, immovable, and therefore unchangeable constellation of figures and architecture. The figures in the
symmetrical rows are often seen in profile and they are
generally directed inward towards the emperor at the
center. The emperor himself, on the other hand, is represented frontally and thus directed out of the relief; he
interrupts the narrative continuity just as the God-Emper-
or himself is placed above the life of mortals, and just as
the imperial ceremonial isolates him in a divine image
raised above the world of the living. The very essence

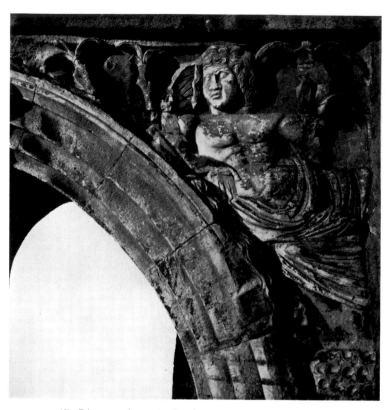

47. River god on Arch of Constantine, A.D. 312-315

of the *dominus* is expressed in this arrangement: his central position in the state, the dependence and subordination of all citizens on him, his superhuman nature. Here is created a compositional scheme expressing the *maiestas domini*, which was to be of fundamental importance for the official art of Late Antiquity and the Middle Ages.

Let us choose as an example of this scheme the famous silver emperor-image in Madrid, representing the Emperor Theodosius enthroned between his co-emperors, Valentinian and Arcadius (Fig. 24). It is not the laws of life and nature which are at work in the grouping of these figures and in their placement within architecture and space. A new order has replaced that of life and nature, a kind of crystallic order: the whole complex of forms is symmetrized around the supernaturally large figure of Theodosius, the groups of figures on both sides arise pyramidally towards him, and pyramidally the gable gathers the architecture around him. The whole Emperor-ideology of Late Antiquity, the sacred absolutism has become evident in this transformation and spiritualization of natural form. The Emperor is God himself on earth. He is the center in a kind of superhuman symmetry, he is the apex of the pyramid of the hierarchy of the state. The emperor-image is a devotional picture.

The church took over this compositional scheme from the state. As an example we illustrate a sarcophagus in Milan, from ca. 400 (Fig. 50). Here it is Christ who is placed at the center, raised high above his surroundings, and here it is the Apostles who are disposed in symmetric rows beneath the central figure. And again this central figure breaks through human context: while the Apostles are facing Christ, Christ is facing frontally toward the viewer like a cult statue to be worshiped. The higher static order, which in the imperial images on the Arch of Constantine are imposed upon the human world, is in the image of Christ sublimated into an expression of the transcendent beauty and regularity of the Kingdom of God. Just as the Emperor in *Liberalitas* made a donation to the people, so also Christ in our relief; but Constantine gave a gift of money to the Roman citizens, Christ gives to all humanity the *nova lex* of the Christian world order (the book-roll in Christ's left hand, presented to Peter). And as the citizens in *Liberalitas* receive the gift with one hand lifted in acclamation, so also the Apostles around Christ: but the citizens are giving thanks for a gift of money, the Apostles are rejoicing in a celestial gift of grace. While, finally, the Emperor is raised up upon a historic tribune, so Christ is elevated

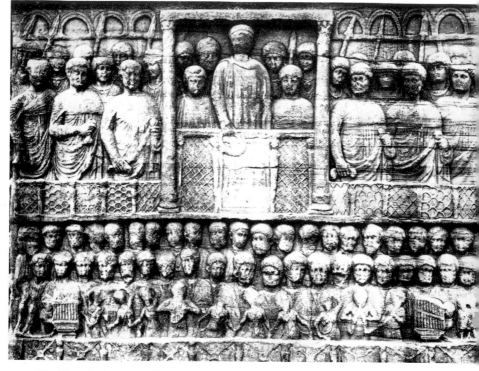

48. Theodosius presiding at circus games. Relief at base of Theodosius Obelisk Constantinople hippodrome. End of IV cent.

to the Mount of Paradise, with the jewel-adorned walls and gates of the Heavenly Jerusalem behind him. *Civitas domini*, which is reflected in the buildings of Forum Romanum surrounding Constantine, has become *civitas Dei*.

The Christian expression of supernatural transcendence in these row formations and symmetries becomes ever more manifest—with the intensification of the mystic—in the development of Late Antique and Early Christian art. We reproduce as an example the apse mosaic in Santa Maria in Domnica in Rome (Fig. 51): Christ between Archangels and Apostles in an upper zone, and the Infant Christ on Mary's lap surrounded by throngs of angels in the apse vault below (817-824).

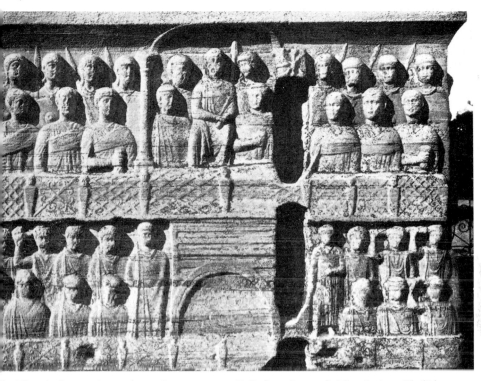

9. Theodosius enthroned at circus games. Relief at base of Theodosius Obelisk, Constantinople hippodrome. End of IV cent.

PORTRAIT SCULPTURE

Throughout the first three centuries of the Empire the Roman portraits, in continuation of the Hellenistic portrait tradition, seek *always*—however different the stylistic currents may be—to convey personal individuality: and this individuality is *always*, still in continuation of the Hellenistic portrait tradition, "life-like," that is, endowed with a natural, animated countenance. Portrait sculpture from the first three centuries of the Empire presents, therefore, *lifelike individuals*. Around A.D. 300 a fundamental change took place in this form of portraiture.[16]

[16] Fundamental for the history of portraiture in Late Antiquity is R. Delbrück, *Spätantike Kaiserporträts*, Berlin, 1933. A good account

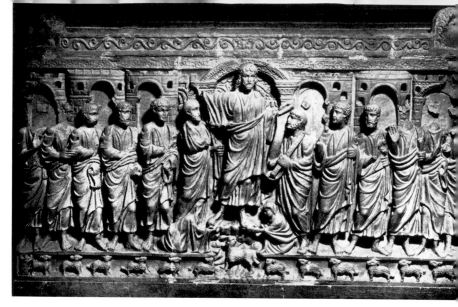

50. Paleochristian sarcophagus, Sant'Ambrogio in Milan. End of IV cent.

Let us take as our point of departure the peculiarly anxiety-filled, glimmeringly mobile portraits from the middle of the third century. The intention is not only to render the individual physiognomic features, but also to represent them in the movement of life. To a degree unparalleled in ancient art the whole personality is caught in a snapshot, in transitory movement, in a sudden glimpse. Thus also the realistic determination of time is introduced in portraiture. The image does not only intend to give the objective physiognomical forms, it also aims at revealing them in time, in the very movement of life, at depicting the play of features in the nervous face, the very flash of personality. Take, for example, the quivering, lifelike image in a sculpture characteristic of this period, for instance the marvelous portrait

of the development in the portrait of Late Antiquity is given by G. von Kaschnitz Weinberg, "Spät-römische Porträts," *Die Antike*, 2, 1926, pp. 36 ff. A broad collection of chronologically arranged material on the history of portraiture from the middle of the third to the end of the fifth century is given in my above-mentioned work, *Studien zur Geschichte des spätantiken Porträts*, Oslo, 1933.

of the Emperor Decius (Fig. 52) in Oslo (249-251). The sideways turning of the head expresses movement, and so does the entire facial composition. Notice the stress that is laid upon asymmetrical constellations of folds and wrinkles, especially striking in the muscles of the forehead and round the mouth with their violent, undulating furrows. Such asymmetries do away with all sorts of stability, firmness, and permanence of form, creating, one might say, a physiognomic situation, only fleetingly possible and bound to change every moment— that is, a constellation suggesting movement. The forehead, for instance, is furrowed by deep but sketchy traces of the chisel: not the furrows themselves as permanently existing lines, but the play of light in them when moving like shifting shadows over the forehead. This also is true for hair and beard: not a plastic chiseling of the individual locks of hair, but a pointillistic hatching and stippling of the forms, so that only at a distance and under the play of light does one get the illusion of hair. It is a technique principally reckoning with the same optic effects as did the impressionistic color decomposi-

51. Apse mosaic in Santa Maria in Domnica, Rome, A.D. 817-824

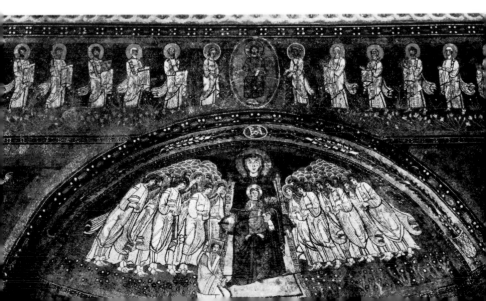

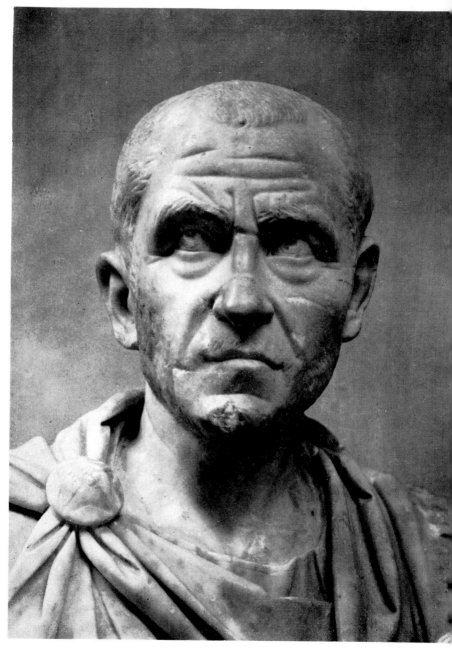

52. Portrait bust of Decius, private collection, Oslo. A.D. 249-251

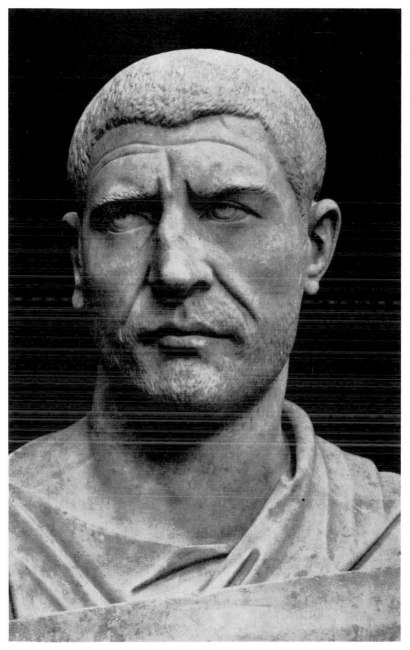

53. Portrait bust of Philippus Arabs, A.D. 244-249, Vatican

tion of the last century, and in both cases the new il-
lusionistic style springs from the older more plastic sense
of form. The development follows the same line as in
the nineteenth century: impressionism develops from the
older realism.

This impressionism, culminating towards the middle
of the third century, has produced some of the greatest
achievements in ancient portraiture. A thrilling human
document is the portrait of Philipus Arabs (244-249)
(Fig. 53). With a great simplifying touch the artist has
managed to concentrate physiognomic life in *one* characteristic sweep. The central motif is the threatening lower-
ing of the brows, corresponding to convulsions of the
forehead muscles and responding to nervous contractions
of the muscles of the mouth. The psychological picture
achieves an almost uncanny intensity. Behind the quivering features the very expression seems to change and
move, flashing like a flickering flame over the face.

Such portraits represent, as we have said, the Roman
art that dominates the period around the middle of the
third century. We find here an impressionism able to
capture in marble the very movement of reality, the very
shifting fluctuations of psychic life. In the course of two
generations, however, this art was totally transformed,
its seething life had vanished in abstraction (Figs. 61,
62). The face no longer vibrates in the current stream of
time; the features suddenly stiffen in an expressive
Medusa-like mask. The inner life—a life beyond space
and time—has been stamped in its large and immovable
features.

How can one explain this radical change in the portrait
form and intention in the latter part of the third century?
Impressionism itself, we may answer, produced—in Antiquity as in modern times—the artistic means, rendering
possible the break-through of the new form. To give

an intense and spontaneous illusion of living, moving reality, form was accentuated so that it fluctuated entirely according to its expressive power, its possibility of giving life in motion. One availed oneself of a decompositional technique reducing plastic values into optical ones and dissolving reality in an illusionary glimmer. The artist thus obtained in the very service of reality, a constantly increasing liberty in relation to the exact details of it. And thereby infinite new possibilities were opened. In the last generation of the third century the overaccentuation of the expressive forms, the dissolving of plastic details, the pointillistic technique becomes ever more predominant. Expression is more and more concentrated in masklike lines. Thus by degrees arises a system of free means of expression, rendering possible a revelation of entirely new psychic contents. These new contents represent the man of Late Antiquity: the inner and spiritual human being, the "pneumatic" personality, to speak in the language of that period. An "abstract" or "expressionistic" portrait, to use the modern term, comes to life.

We select as examples two male heads from shortly before the turn of the third century (Figs. 54, 55). The conflict between the new endeavors and the traditional impressionistic cliché is evident. The abstract articulation of the eyes, the distant glance beyond time, derives from the new aim of expression. But still tradition is at work quivering in momentary life, even though about to stiffen into an abstract serenity which spreads from the eyes to the entire face. The uneasy almost pained movements which run across the surface in asymmetric flickers, are confined in a peculiar way to certain areas of the face, particularly to the muscles of the forehead; they do not emanate from an organic emotion embracing the whole. Thus the physiognomic life is shattered and

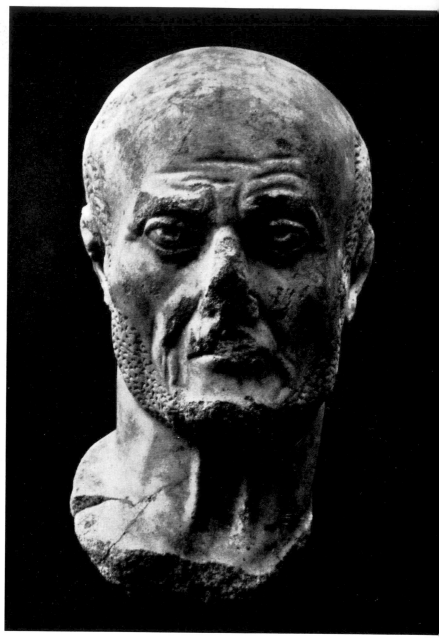

54. Portrait head from end of III cent., National Museum, Naples

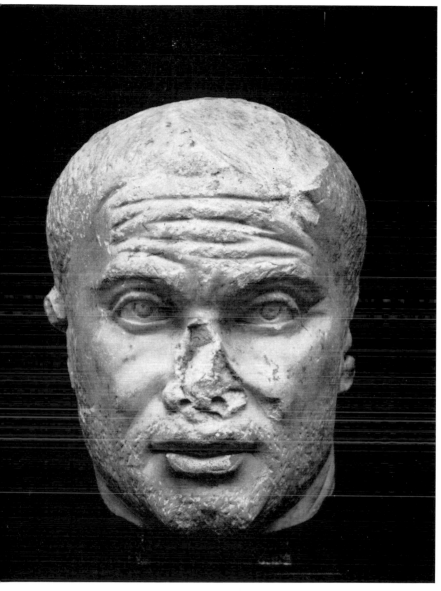

55. Portrait head from end of III cent., Ny Carlsberg Glyptothek,
Copenhagen

burst, the nervous play stiffens into cramps and convulsions. One must compare the peculiar disintegrated compositions and the strange marionette-like movements in the contemporary art of sarcophagi (pp. 88 ff.; Figs. 32-34): a dissolving in the sphere of art which, as we have seen, coincides with the anarchic conditions of the spiritual and material existence of the period (pp. 39 f.).

Contemporaneous with this disintegration of traditional organic form is a new feeling for the compact mass, the "stereometric" form.[17] As examples we reproduce three portrait busts from the period around A.D. 300, one from the Latin, two from the Greek region of the Empire[18] (Figs. 56-60). The same blocklike simplification of the organic form asserts itself everywhere. At the same time there is a weakening of the individualizing facial features; they no longer evolve from deep within a thoroughly articulate head structure, but reside in their own layer on the outside of the block. As demonstrated by coin portraits, this new portrait style first appeared in the eastern part of the Empire;[19] it is first found on coins struck by the mints in Nicomedia, Kyzikos, Antioch, and Alexandria. But the style soon becomes common in all the provinces of the Empire, even though the West Roman and, to an even greater extent, the local Greek portrait always preserves more of the traditional organic form structure. This new, immobile, blocklike form which strikes through physiognomic articulation has its striking parallels in the contemporary cubic palace style (pp. 70 ff.), in the massive wall formations that now absorb the traditional décor in architecture (pp. 16 ff.), in the compact row formations of figurative art (p. 96) —indeed, in the whole militaristic way of life character-

---

[17] L'Orange, *Studien*, p. 37   [18] *Ibid.*, figs. 51-58, 64.
[19] *Ibid.*, p. 25.

istic of the period, which makes individuals disappear into columns and squares (pp. 7 f.).

Characteristic of the development throughout the following decades is an increasingly regular and more statuesque block form as illustrated by a porphyry portrait (Fig. 61) of an emperor in the museum in Cairo.[20] The structure of the head and the features of the face are confined within large, clearly defined flat or curved planes, individual forms, such as wrinkles, furrows, locks of hair, become more and more firmly symmetrized according to the vertical axis of the face. It is thus again, as we saw in the reliefs, a sort of mechanical way of planning the modeling which replaces the organic way that had already disintegrated.[21]

The portrait in Cairo is of Eastern origin and more advanced in the new tendency than West Roman portraits. But these also follow, as has been indicated, the same line of development. A late tetrarchic portrait in the Vatican (Fig. 62) and the famous Dogmatius portrait in the Lateran (Fig. 63), dated by an inscription to the late Constantinian period (A.D. 323-337), demonstrate two steps in the advancing process of stereometric crystallization in western Roman art. The impressionistic glimmer, the fleeting asymmetries in the skin and muscular surface are smoothed out. All the creases in muscle and skin are simplified in clear, regular strokes. The eye no longer flickers, but rests immobile upon a point in the distance. In the portrait of Dogmatius we find the full stereometric simplification of the whole complex of form and the strict symmetric subordination of all the individual forms according to the central axis of the face.

[20] R. Delbrück, *Antike Porphyrwerke*, Berlin, 1932, pp. 92 f., pls. 38 f. L'Orange, *Studien*, pp. 22 ff., figs. 42, 44.

[21] L'Orange, *op.cit.*, pp. 21 f., 53 f., 56, 64 f. A. Riegl, *Spätröm. Kunstindustrie*, pp. 48 f., Vienna, 1901-1923.

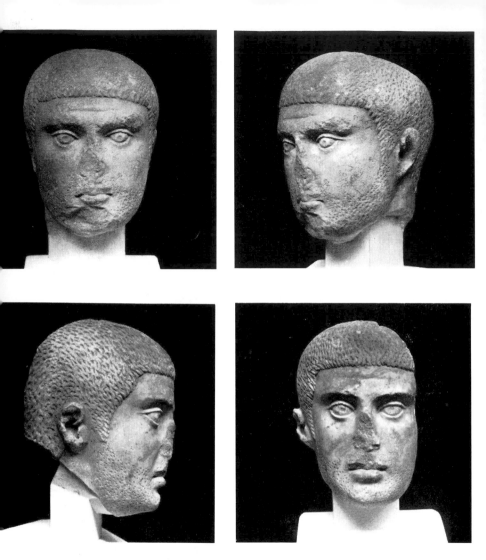

56-59. Two portrait heads from ca. A.D. 300, National Museum, Athens

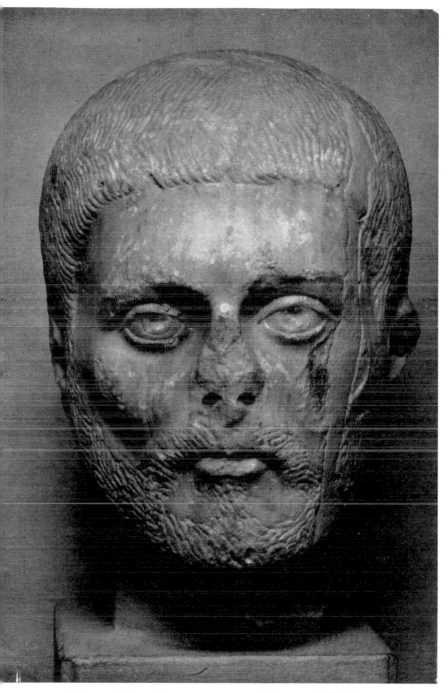

60. Portrait head from ca. A.D. 300, Museum of Bardo

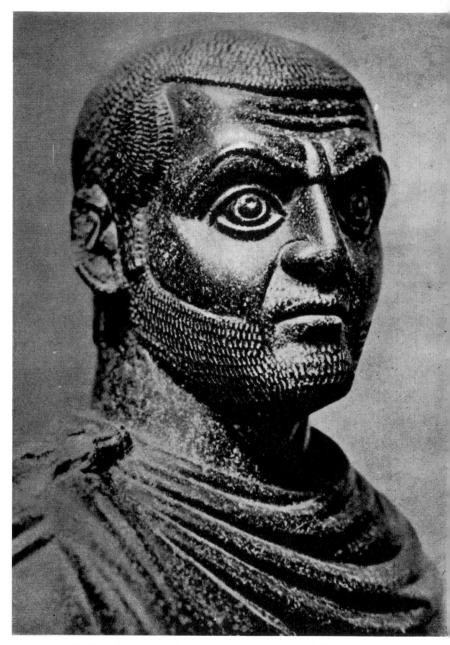

61. Porphyry portrait bust of an emperor, probably Licinius,
A.D. 307-323, Museum of Cairo

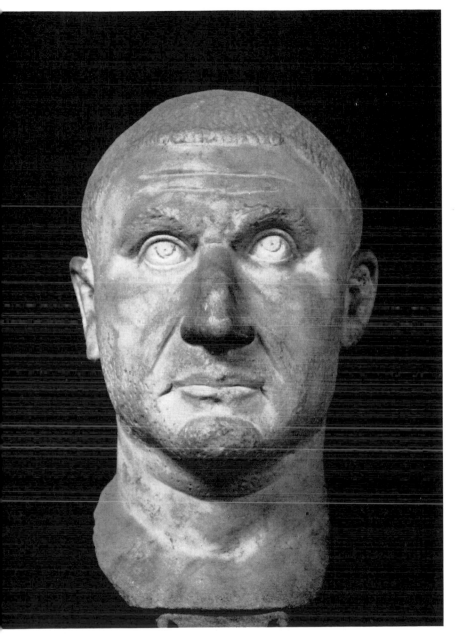

62. Portrait head from the late Tetrarchy, Vatican

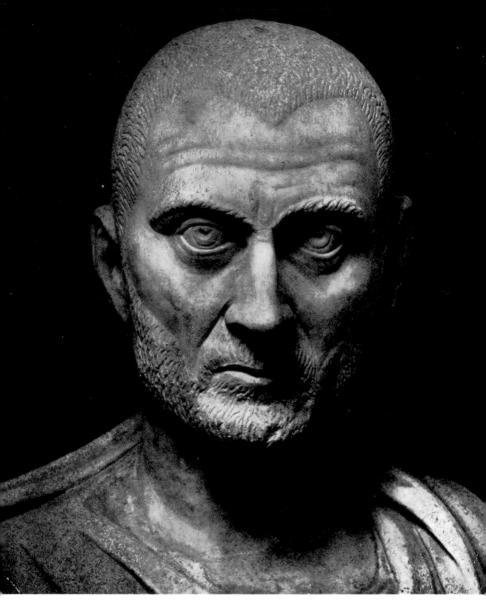

63. Head of portrait statue of Dogmatius, A.D. 323-377, Lateran, Rome

The cap of hair is outlined by mathematically regular contours with the point of its "widow's peak" in the axis, the furrows of the forehead undulate in severe parallel curves, the eyes are framed by concentric arches. Instead of the quivering life of the surface a crystallic reflection of the inner abstract life. No longer the flashing play of features, but a permanent expressive mask. In this mask the eyes in their frame of intensifying curves dominate the total expression.

As the vivid organic nature now gives way to a very firm regularity, so the individual to the type. We have seen in the portrayal of saints (pp. 24 ff.) how the natural human features yield to a higher stereotypy which characterizes the unchangeable nature of the holy and indicates their position in an eternal hierarchical order. The saints, therefore, appear identical. A similar stereotypy also asserts itself, beginning with the tetrarchic period, in the portrayal of the emperors. We have listened to the panegyrist's praise of the *similitudo* of Diocletian and Maximian (pp. 46 ff.). And we hear further how this ideal similarity rests upon their common divine essence. An unchangeable "holy type" (p. 50) permeates all earthly chance and marks the facial features of the God-Emperors.

However, it was not the emperor-image of the Tetrarchy which was to become definitive in the sacred typology of the Empire. It was Constantine's universal monarchy (from 324), heir to the Tetrarchy, which in its emperor image was to create the lasting emperor ideal. The type emerges with such portraits as the colossal head of Constantine in the Palazzo dei Conservatori in Rome, which originally surmounted the enormous statue of the enthroned emperor in his Basilica at Forum Romanum (Fig. 64). The head faces front, originally in the axis of the basilica. It is built up by clearly defined planes

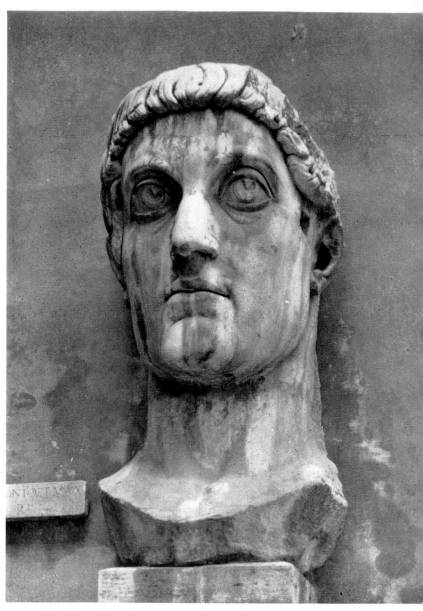

64. Colossal head of Constantine, Palazzo dei Conservatori, Rome

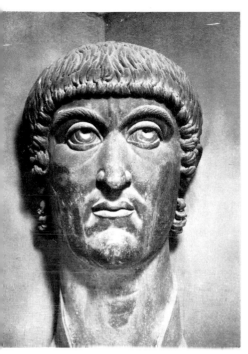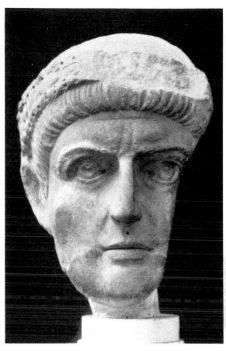

65. Colossal bronze head of emperor, probably Constantius II,
A.D. 323-361, Palazzo dei Conservatori, Rome
66. Imperial portrait from v cent. A.D., Ny Carlsberg Glyptothek,
Copenhagen

that are outlined by geometrically regular curves, the
separate elements submit to the strict symmetry around
the center axis of the face; the cranium is rounded dome-
like, the hair closes about the forehead and temples in a
complete archivolt of locks where the center lock is the
keystone; the eyes, eyelids, and eyebrows conform to the
system of concentric arches and curve one above another,
arcade over arcade. Every movement has subsided. The
features, the whole face rests firmly within the imperturbable order of eternity.

The eyes, being supernaturally large and wide-open
and framed by the accentuated concentric curves of the
deepcut lids and brows, express more clearly than ever

the transcendence of the ruler's personality. In this gaze he travels far beyond his physical surroundings and attains his goal in a higher sphere, in contact and identity with the governing powers. Providence in person, the irresistible controller of fate, *fatorum arbiter*, rises before us, with all the future on his knees. The imperial ideology of the time is crystallized in this face. It makes us think of those representative scenes in art or in life, where the emperor appears as judge of the world, as cosmocrator, as μοῖρα and *fatum*. His throne is set in the hub of the universe, he is the very law of cosmic motion, *rector totius orbis*, with the wheel of the zodiac in his hand. The head is an expression of the emperor's divine power, his *divina maiestas*, rather than a portrait of an individual man. We are confronted with the "holy countenance" of this power, and we experience ourselves the significance and reality of such terms as *sacer vultus, sacrum os, divinus vultus*, generally applied to the effigy of the emperors of Late Antiquity (compare Figs. 65, 66).[22]

Do we not perceive, we ask in the end, behind this image type, the solemn ritual style in the personal appearance of the emperor? Do we not receive a glimpse of the ceremonial symmetry around the emperor's immobile figure—around this glittering *caeleste miraculum* described in contemporary sources? The living emperor appears in a peculiar statuesque way, monumentally elevated over the world of mortals. Ammianus Marcellinus (16,10) has drawn a famous picture of Constantius II on his entry into Rome—a picture of the living Emperor which can be compared to the imperial portrait-type we have been studying. "He looked so stiffly ahead as if he had an iron band about his neck and he turned his face neither to the right nor to the left, he was not as a

[22] L'Orange, *Apotheosis in Ancient Portraiture*, Oslo, 1947, pp. 116 ff.

living person, but as an image." (*Nec dextra vultum, nec laeva flectebat; tamquam figmentum hominis.*) This hieratic emperor style, which, as an expression of *divina maiestas*, in the same way leaves its mark upon palace (pp. 73 ff.), image, and living reality, can furthermore be traced through Byzantium all the way down to the Holy Russian Empire. With words that in a striking way remind us of Ammianus', Bertel Gripenberg recounts his childhood impressions of Alexander III: "He stared straight ahead, and his features were as immovable as those of a statue. A man of stone, a personification of power and fate."[23]

[23] A. Boëthius has collocated these striking parallel passages. B. Gripenberg, *Det var de tiderna*, quoted from A. Boëthius in *Svenska Dagbladet*, 4.5. 1944. Cf. O. Treitinger, *Die ostRöm. Kaiser und Reichsidee*, Jena, 1938, p. 235.

CONCLUSION

IN THIS study we have attempted to demonstrate how the disintegration of society under the Principate and the establishment of a new order under the Dominate were accompanied by a parallel break-up and reorganization in the world of art. We have, for instance, seen how the new "block-style" in art emerged contemporary with the formation of massive structures in the state and community, and how in both contexts the traditional individualization and articulation of the various elements were gradually reduced or disappeared altogether.

Such a correspondence between the structure of the state and the forms in art would be easy to comprehend if the arts were directed by the state and if the stylistic form, so to speak, were derived from the state itself as a reflection of the state system and as a servant of the state's intentions. As we have seen, however, the new language of art forms emerged *spontaneously*, as a result of a profound logical development within art itself, and not simply by mirroring the development in another sector of human activity, although it may also be true that reciprocal influences between the various activities were present and played their part in the total development. The new solutions in architecture and art were, as we have seen, at each step the result of a natural development of certain stylistic predispositions of the preceding artistic situation, as the consequence of special qualities inherent in the material itself. The similarity between the form of practical organization and that of free art was thus based upon a deeper identity than that of a simple reflection: namely, upon the need of a specific mentality for identical form in all sectors of life; in other words, both the form of practical organization and of free art were the expression of the spiritual mentality of the period.

We can, therefore, speak about autonomous courses of *evolution* and *devolution* which run parallel in both the world of art and society. Thus the disintegrated Empire and the anarchical conditions of the second half of the third century formed, as we have seen, a striking parallel to the "burst" pictures and physiognomically "decomposed" portraits in contemporary art. But just as striking is the parallel between the structure of society and of art during the reaction to the anarchy which followed under Diocletian. And again we see that identical solutions were reached, not as a reflection, but independently of each other. They emerged as a logical consequence of particular qualities inherent in each of the two spheres of human activity. The new tetrarchical order of state which grew up as the solution to the acute political situation, showed in its characteristic features symmetry, row formations, mechanical coordination—exactly the same pattern of composition that became dominant in contemporary art. But also in art, this pattern of composition was a solution resulting from the special predispositions within the proper field of form during the previous period. It is the spontaneous reaction to the "burst" type of composition—the disjointed pictorial elements cry for a new order.

Should we summarize the basic characteristics of the structural change taking place in the transition from Principate to Dominate they would appear perhaps with greatest clarity when seen under two aspects: that of massive simplification and that of mechanical crystallization. Let us briefly sum up our investigation under these two aspects.

To the massive, all-absorbing formations in the life of

state and society correspond the distinctive compact form creations in contemporary architecture and art. Here also the individual articulations disappear into immovable blocklike solids. We have seen in portrait sculpture how the decline in the plastic differentiation of the form corresponded to a new feeling for the solid mass. The block form which here breaks through the physiognomical features has its striking parallels in the contemporary cubic palace style and the solid wall formations which now absorb the traditional decoration in architecture. And everywhere the block tends towards crystallized regularity and static repose.

In the whole of conceptual life there is a movement away from the complex towards the simple, from the mobile towards the static, from the dialectic and relative towards the dogmatic and the authoritarian, from the empirical towards theology and theosophy. There is a trend towards plain, uncomplicated absolutes which are imperturbably fixed in themselves. In this way the historical victory tends, as we have seen, to become "the eternal victory"; the historical victor to become the absolute victor, "the universal victor," "the victor over all people." When actions or things are embodied in such absolutes, their individual outlines and their adaptability to situations, everything relative, dialectical, and mobile, disappear; they all become alike and come to rest in this similarity.

In the same way figurative art moves away from the animated forms of nature towards a firm and unflexible typology, from plastic articulation to conceptual image, from body to symbol. The concrete representation of nature is forced into a simplified, idealized image and comes to rest within this image. Thus, as we have seen in the depiction of saints and emperors, the individual human features give way to a higher order of types which

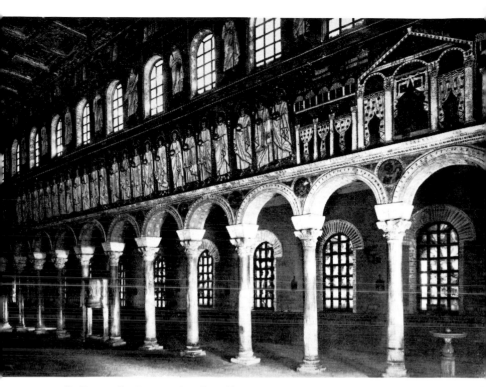

67. Row of saints in Sant'Apollinare Nuovo, Ravenna

characterizes the immutable essence of the holy one. Here is a sacral stereotypy which fixes the divine essence of emperors and saints and at the same time indicates their place in an unalterable hierarchical order.

A static world of types and eternal orders: it is towards this—cutting through our diverse and changeable reality—that Late Antiquity's transcendent glance is directed. In this way art tries to capture the exalted, unchangeable regularities behind the shifting multiplicity of our world. A fixed, mechanical coordination replaces the free groupings in earlier art. In the large relief compositions the free space around the figures disappears; they lose their mobility. At the same time the figures are usually placed in rows with an infinite repetition of identical elements (Fig. 67). And this system is made even firmer by the

Conclusion

rows of identical elements or pairs of identical elements being symmetrized around a fixed center. The greatest solidity in the static system is achieved when the main axes of the composition are made parallel to the framework, whereby all the pictorial elements are fixed within a geometrical coordinate system.

A similar placing of the contents within an immovable static order is brought about with the systematizing of belief and teaching, which during Late Antiquity totally changes the manifold religiousness and dialectical wisdom of Antiquity. The Neo-Platonism after Plotinus becomes a speculative theology which combines the various classical cults into a systematic whole and brings religious movement, with the exception of Christianity, to a standstill. The philosophical theology of "the Hellenistic Scholastic" Proclos (A.D. 410-485) marks the final point of this process. The religions and philosophical doctrines of Antiquity arise with fossilized authority in his all-embracing system which transforms the Greek world of ideas into a "hierarchy of mythologemes."[1] Also in the doctrines of Christian teaching the theological dialectic of earlier times gives way to increasingly authoritarian and immovable conceptions.[2] During the third and fourth centuries, on the basis of the theology of Clemens and Origenes, a constantly more systematic elaboration of doctrine takes place, which in the end is crystallized into the Catholic dogma. As we have seen, the characteristic Late Antique endeavor of the Christian Empire, to bring the whole religious life under the fixed norms of a "state church," is already apparent under Aurelian and the Tetrarchy.

[1] W. Windelband - A. Goedeckemeyer, *Geschichte der abendländischen Philosophie im Altertum* (Handb. d. klass. Altertumswiss., v, I, I, 1923), Munich, 1923, p. 295.

[2] A. von Harnack, *Grundriss der Dogmengeschichte*, pp. 150, 209, 232 f., 235. Windelband-Goedeckemeyer, *op.cit.*, pp. 301, 284 ff.

130

Conclusion

Thus, in all fields of human endeavor the process of *evolution* and *devolution* tends towards simplified, massive, and at the same time statically fixed forms. Is it not as if life itself, during this great, dangerous, all-encompassing metamorphosis leading from Antiquity to the Middle Ages, armors and encloses itself in these massive blocks and unbreakable rigid systems in the spheres of state, art, and religion? Thus Rome and Constantinople and behind the *limes* the whole Roman Empire, at this period literally armored and enclosed themselves within the hard shell of the most powerful fortifications of Antiquity. Is it not as if life itself, both of the spirit and of the body, sacrificed liberty and mobility to security and permanence? Who knows if the seed could have survived without this firm shell.